BULLDOGS

AN OWNER'S COMPANION

Christian Bruton

The Crowood Press

First published in 1998 by
The Crowood Press Ltd
Ramsbury, Marlborough
Wiltshire SN8 2HR

British Library Cataloguing-in-Publication Data
A catalogue record for this book is available from the British Library.

ISBN 1 86126 134 9

Dedication
Dedicated to my darling grandmother Clara Nielson and my partner David
McHale, the most loyal friends I could ever have.

Acknowledgements
I should like to thank Maggie Story, surely the greatest secretary of the world's
greatest club, and the Incorporated for all their help and co-operation, and for
allowing me access to such rare and valuable photos. I am very grateful to Neil
Stone for all his comprehensive research on the Australian scene, to Helene Denis
on the French Club, Pauline Horner for the research on homoeopathy, to Simon
Lathan for his photographic skills and to Ray Knudson for his help on the
American scene. Lastly to Elizabeth Mallard-Shaw, editor extraordinaire for her
frugal pruning.

Picture credits
Black and white photographs taken and/or supplied by the author, except where
stated otherwise.

Line-drawings by the author.

Photograph page 4: 'Yer does me credit.' Postcard produced before the Second
World War.

Typeface used: Palatino.

Typeset by D & N Publishing
Membury Business Park, Lambourn Woodlands, Hungerford, Berkshire.

Printed and bound in Great Britain by Redwood Books, Trowbridge, Wiltshire

Contents

Preface

Contrary to popular belief, Sir Winston Churchill never owned a Bulldog; in fact he kept Miniature Poodles. Yet, one of this century's shrewdest politicians was quick to latch on to and utilize the British identification with the courage and loyalty of the breed that represents unbroken tradition, stability and patriotism. Most political parties have had trysts with the breed at some stage or another, all wishing to associate themselves with his virtues of tenacity, steadfastness and courage. And for countless years he was always portrayed alongside John Bull, resplendent in his Union Jack waistcoat, a national hero.

Over the years, various manufacturers have used the image of the Bulldog to promote their products or connect them with the qualities that are exemplified in the breed. Perhaps the most famous of them is Mack Trucks.

Mack Trucks used a Bulldog named Thunder, who belonged to a member of the Detroit Bulldog Club. He was selected by an advertising agency from an array of large dogs, to represent the 'massive' image that Mack wanted to project. At seventy-eight pounds (35kg), Thunder was perfect for the role. Also in the States, five universities – the University of Georgia, Yale, Butler University Indianapolis, Fresno State, and Minnesota – have adopted the Bulldog as their mascot, as have the United States Marine Corps. and Mississippi State. Closer to home, in 1968, the Royal Navy launched the seventh ship to be called HMS Bulldog, a survey ship.

My own fascination with the breed began quite early on, and by chance. I had always been surrounded by various dogs, and during my early formative years we had an array of different breeds. There was a Corgi that couldn't behave and ended up behind the bar – not behind bars I hasten to add – at the local Royal Oak pub; a Cocker Spaniel that died early of distemper; and there was a cross named Sandy left over from the war who had apparently foregone the indignity of the Anderson shelter and consequently was to be found comfortably covered in glass splinters each morning when the family surfaced – both parties apparently sharing a mutual disappointment that the other had survived.

My Aunt Christina had a passion for Basset Hounds, which she loved and showed for many years, and with some success, under her Seven Hills affix. When I was about eleven years old she presented the family with a lemon-and-white Basset Hound puppy, and we named him Oliver. Oliver was quite oversized and, although extremely dim, he managed to be possibly slightly more eccentric a puppy than I was a child. In any event it was deemed my job to walk him each day, a task that I religiously carried out, if sometimes under duress.

Most days I would cross paths with a neighbour who had just bought a beautiful white-ticked Bulldog whose name was Adam. Being a typical hound, Oliver had little interest in people, and he would pick up a scent and stray for miles in Richmond Park. Adam the Bulldog, on the other hand, saw no point for such a pointless exercise and was much happier to sit with me while the park police rounded up Oliver. I was so charmed by Adam that when, a few years later, the landlord of a local pub was looking for a new home for his four-year-old male Bulldog, I immediately accepted on behalf of everybody. But it was not to be; on the day my Bulldog was due to arrive, my younger brother brought home a puppy Border Collie, and the Bulldog had to be cancelled.

However, Bulldog ownership was not to evade me for ever. In 1975, while watching Crufts Show on television, David McHale and I were captivated by the appearance of a most magnificent Bulldog, who in hindsight must have been Denis and Barbara Shaw's Ch. Beechlyn Golden Nugget who won the Utility Group and went on to Reserve Best in Show that year. It was ironic that some ten years or so later we stood on that same rostrum with Ch. Tyegarth Jacob of Kelloe, and our names were engraved on the same commemorative trophies.

The following week, we bought a Sunday national newspaper and found a bulldog puppy advertised for sale in Wales. Neither of us had ever seen a bulldog puppy before, and we hadn't a clue what to expect, but Cedric turned out to be an adorable fawn and white puppy who, at about sixteen weeks of age, was only marginally smaller than David's mother Jane, who had come along with us to collect him.

Cedric's arrival precipitated a move to a sensible townhouse with a garden; and my treasured sports car was traded for a sensible hatchback, which couldn't be garaged as we now had grand plans to convert the garage into a kennel. Cedric was soon followed by Keldholme Rosy Primrose, a white brindle pied bitch bred from Arthur Westlake's

'Baytor' and Pete Truman's 'Mantru' kennels. She was a beautiful Bulldog, if a little undersize, and our first championship show exhibit. We named her after Wallis Simpson. Wallis was entered at Darlington – in those days the world's largest one-day championship show – where she took third place in a large Junior Class (under breed specialist Margaret Chambers), qualifying her for Crufts. We were elated. Some years later, the same judge was to award Jacob his second CC at Leeds Championship Show.

At this time we began to look around for a show-quality male. At a social night organized by the London Bulldog Society we met Pat Dellar of Merriveen fame, who had enjoyed a great success in other breeds before coming into Bulldogs. Through her we met Sheila Cartwright, who had just recently brought her beautiful bitch, Tyegarth Gabrielle, to Pat's (later to be legendary) stud-dog, Ch. Merriveen Happy Daze. Gabrielle's litter consisted of several dogs and two red-and-white bitches. Sheila always registered her Bulldog litters with biblical names, selected in alphabetical order. Whether she had reared ten litters in Bulldogs by this stage I do not know but she had worked her way up to the letter J. So the remaining boys were Tyegarth Joseph and Tyegarth Jacob, the bitches Tyegarth Jezebel and Tyegarth Judith. We chose Jacob, and later, Pat Meredith (Pat Dellars's kennel maid) purchased Joseph.

Jacob went through some really strange stages during his development. As you will read in later chapters this is typical, but it all came more than right. Our top show stock have included Ch. Tyegarth Jacob of Kelloe (34 CCs), Ch. Tyegarth Lucifer (4 CCs), Ch. Brenuth Britannia of Kelloe (4 CCs), Ch. Maid Available of Kelloe (9 CCs), Ch. Kelloe White Glove (50 CCs), Ch. Kelloe Maid in Silver (4 CCs), Ch. Kelloe Kid Glove (4 CCs), Ch. Kelloe Angel Dust (4 CCs), Ch. Kelloe Truly Madly Deeply (4 CCs), and Ch. Medbull Gold Dust Over Kelloe (13 CCs).

Although my Bulldogs have enjoyed meteoric success, when at home – whether they be a multiple CC winning champion, or purely a pet, a baby puppy or an oldy – they are all treated as treasured, much loved and valued members of the family. Of the twelve ticket-winning Bulldogs I have campaigned, ten champions have shared eighteen Utility Groups, three best in shows and five reserve best in shows at all-breed general championship shows. My dogs have also won Best in Show at The Bulldog Club Incorporated Show, The British Club Show, The Junior, in fact at every premier club show, amassing over 130 CCs, including Crufts on three occasions.

Of the three greatest Bulldogs of all time – Ch. Beechlyn Golden Nugget of Denbrough. Ch. Tyegarth Jacob of Kelloe and Ch. Kelloe White Glove – I have the honour to have owned two and bred the latter.

Although these achievements have been tremendous fun, enabling me to mix with royalty, pop stars and celebrities, as well as travel the world, I have always felt that the breed is bigger than any individual and should never be used as a vehicle for self-promotion or financial gain. We are all but caretakers of this most wonderful, if difficult of breeds. If we can continue to breed to the Standard, preserve the unique temperament, and improve the general health aspect, we have done as much as can be expected. Join me and all Bulldog lovers worldwide in our sincere wish to leave the leading aristocrat of pedigree dogs in a much healthier, more stable way, and in the hands of the caring, loving and responsible people that they most surely deserve.

Chris Bruton 1998

1

The History of the Breed

The celebrated breeder, judge and writer Enno Meyer once wrote that of all domestic animals, the Bulldog probably represents the greatest departure from nature's original plan for a canine. He added that while at no time has the breed enjoyed a real peak of popularity, it has held a steady and consistent following in the fancy.

It is impossible to include here a precise, fully comprehensive history of the Bulldog. However, I shall endeavour to outline the main factors that influenced the breed and contributed to its development through the centuries.

Early Beginnings

Palaeontologists believe that the origins of the dog go back some fifty-five million years, and that it may have originally shared common ancestry with the bear. The modern domesticated dog is the result of three distinct types: the giant bear-dogs; the extinct hyena-type dogs of North America and its related group, the wolf-like hunting dogs of India and Africa; and then wolves, wild dogs and foxes, which are considered to be the direct ascendants of the domesticated dog.

Dogs are referred to fourteen times in the Bible, including Genesis, references which attest to the ancient and enduring nature of the relationship that exists between man and dog. Historical records of huge Dane-like dogs appear in early Assyrian bas-reliefs, and in Egyptian, Greek and Roman friezes. When the seafaring Phoenicians came to the south west of England to trade for Cornish tin, they brought with them the fierce Mollossian dogs of the ancient Greeks, and Assyrian or Asiatic mastiffs. A jawbone from this period, found in a cave deposit at Glamorgan, Wales, resembles that of either a Tibet Mastiff or African Lycaon Hound and has been described as the jawbone of a Bulldog.

The Phoenicians were followed by the Greeks, Belgae and then the Romans, all eager for the rich natural resources of Britain. Many believe the Bulldog to be a descendant of the fierce war-dogs, such as those that ran alongside the scythed chariots of Queen Boudicca. The Romans were quick to appreciate these early British dogs, many of whom were to end their days in the amphitheatres of Rome. Realizing the superiority of such dogs over their own, they applied the name of Mollossi as nothing inferior could possibly emanate from Rome.

In the eighth century, the Roman Gratius Faliscus wrote of the 'Pugnaces of Britain', which existed in two distinct groups: a large type used in hunting and fighting large beasts, and a smaller guard-dog type for protecting home and flocks. The latter is generally considered to have been the foundation stock of today's Bulldog. Earlier still, another Roman, Claudian (AD 395–404), wrote, 'The British Hound that brings the bull's big forehead to the ground'; and Symmachus, a contemporary, mentions seven Irish Bulldogs presented to the throng at Rome. These dogs were greatly admired by the people, who were so awestruck by their ferocity and boldness that it was rumoured the only way they could be imported was bound in iron cages.

From Bandog to Bulldog

On St Brice's day, 13 November 1209, the Earl of Warren witnessed from his castle ramparts at Stamford, Lincolnshire, an enraged bull being harassed in the castle meadow by a pack of butchers' dogs. The panic-stricken bull ran amok through the streets of the nearby town, still chased by the dogs. So delighted was the Earl with the display that he gave the meadow to the town's butchers with the stipulation that a similar fight be staged each year on the first day of Advent, thus to open the preparations for Christmas. And so started the period of bull- and bear-baiting contests that lasted for more than six centuries.

Throughout the Middle Ages, the breed is commonly thought to have shared its identity with the early mastiffs; in fact the name mastiff seems to heave been applied indiscriminately to most large or giant dogs. Other popular names were allan, alaunts or bandogs. These were taught to bite and hang onto the bull's ears, but later to bite into the bull's most tender and sensitive part, his nose. It was as bandogs that they were mentioned in the works of Geoffrey Chaucer and by 1500 the breed was being referred to as *Bondogge* or *Boldogge*.

In 1576 Dr Johannes Caius, writing probably the first complete work on native breeds, gives the reason for these names:

... them are tied up in chaines and strong bonds in the dai time for doing hurt abroad, which is a huge dog, stubborn, ouglie, eager, burdenouse of bodie, and therefore of little swiftness, terrible and fearful to behold and oftentimes more fierce and fell than anie Archadian Curr.

Dr Caius continues: 'they are taught to bait the bear, the bull, the lion, and other such cruel and bloudie beasts,' and that the *Bondogge* is 'serviceable against fox and badger, to drive wild and tame swine out of meadows.' The *Bondogge* or *Bandogge* is mentioned by Shakespeare in *King Henry V1* and continues to appear in literature and works of art such as in the *Boar and Stag Hunt* by Rubens.

Bull-Running

The precedent set at Stamford developed over the years into an appalling spectacle, and persons of the baser sort, such as horse-jobbers, hostlers, butcher- and pig-jobbers diverged on the town each year in large numbers. There was rioting and yelling, and at the tolling of the bell, the bull was let loose from the dark shed in which the unfortunate creature had been detained overnight. If the bull's ferocity didn't meet with the mob's approval, the poor beast's flesh was lacerated and spirit poured into the wounds. Bullards were employed to incite the bull to stampede at a furious rate through the town; then they drove the frenzied animal on to the bridge, where it was surrounded and lifted over the parapet to plunge into the river below. (From this dreadful custom came the phrase 'tossing the bull over the bridge' as another term for foul play.) If this was all accomplished before twelve noon, the townsmen were entitled to another bull.

In Staffordshire, at Tutbury Castle, John O'Gaunt, Duke of Lancaster (1340–1399) instituted another form of 'bull-running', possibly to please his Spanish wife, Constanza of Castile, by imitating the bulls feasts of her native land. The bailiff of the manor was obliged to provide a bull for the castle minstrels. A proclamation was posted demanding that all persons except the minstrels, give way to the bull and not come within forty feet of him (a request that I am sure most were only too keen to comply with). The bull then had the tips of his horns sawn off, his ears and tail cut off, and his nose blown full of pepper. The Prior's bailiff would then unleash the bull amongst the minstrels. If any of them could cut off a piece of the bull's skin before he ran into neighbouring Derbyshire, that minstrel was declared King of Music and the bull was his. But the poor bull was in a no-win situation, for if it managed to reach Derbyshire uncut he was the property

11

'The Baited Bull Broke Loose' taken from Edgar Farman's masterpiece The Bulldog: a Monograph.

of the Lord Prior, who would collar and rope him and then take him to the bull-ring in the High Street, Tutbury, to be baited with dogs.

As the years went by the young men of Staffordshire and Derbyshire, all armed with yard-long sticks, attempted to drive the bull into their adversaries' county, with the result that many sustained broken skulls and other appalling injuries.

Bull-running was abolished in 1778. But while the gruesome custom had been perpetrated in only three towns in England – Stamford in Lincolnshire, Tutbury in Staffordshire, and Tetbury in Gloucestershire – bull-baiting was practised widely throughout the country and continued to be so.

Bull-Baiting

Bull-baiting developed as a universal British sport through the erroneous conviction that baiting before killing made meat more tender than when the bull was slaughtered in the usual manner. It is not only the bulls that suffered as a result of this: the dogs, too, were subjected to appalling cruelty, usually in a bid to arouse their gameness.

One such incident was described in an article in the January 1824 edition of *Sporting Magazine*, about a butcher who took a bitch, accompanied by her litter of puppies, to a bull-bait. As soon as the bitch was unleashed, she immediately pinned the bull to the ground, and this despite having scarcely a tooth in her head. The butcher then cut her to pieces with a hedge-bill, and she only let hold with her last breath. The spectacle instantly created a huge demand for her puppies, which the butcher promptly sold for five guineas apiece. Another harrowing account tells of another man, so confident of the pure blood and courageousness of his dog, that he proposed a wager: he would, at four different intervals during the contest, amputate one of the dog's feet; he maintained that after each deprivation the dog, on his stumps, would continue to attack the bull. All went as predicted, and when the master called him off the dog limped bleeding to his master's arms, who then cut off his head – possibly the most merciful action of that day.

Another writer reported seeing a Bulldog pin down an American bison until the bison brought forward his hind legs and crushed the dog to death. The bison's muzzle, terribly mangled, had to be torn free from the dead dog's mouth. It was a common sight for dogs to continue baiting with their entrails trailing on the ground; often the bulls gored so ferociously that the dog's entire bowels were torn apart. Quite often a Bulldog surrounded by fireworks would be drawn through the crowd, holding tight with his teeth to a sponge attached to a rope. A typical public notice, appearing in the *Weekly Journal*, went as follows:

July 22nd 1721, note: also a bear to be baited and a mad green bull to be turned loose in the gaming place; with fireworks all over him and a comet at his tail, and Bulldogs after him. A dog will be drawn up with fireworks after him in the middle of the yard; and an Ass to be baited upon the same stage.

Boxing matches were sometimes held in conjunction with the bull-baits, and a record 5,000 spectators turned up for such a display at a meeting in 1824.

Bull-baiting took place in rope enclosures inside circular buildings, reminiscent of the old Roman amphitheatres. These were in turn surrounded by kennels built on scaffolding, safely away from the public. The main object was for the dog to 'pin and hold' the bull, usually by his nose – the most tender part – which would normally render the bull helpless. During the fight the bull would lower his head to use his horns, and usually a hole was provided in which to bury his nose. The collar around his neck was fastened to a thick rope of about four to five yards in length, and this was attached via a hook to a stake secured in the ground. The dogs were trained to 'play low', to hold their heads close to the ground and creep along on their bellies to avoid the bull's horns.

The dog began to change shape during this period. With careful breeding, owners were managing to produce an animal with the bulk of his weight near the head so that when the bull shook him there was less chance of the dog's back being broken. Originally, the forerunners of the Bulldog – such as mastiffs and Bull Terriers – were used, but they were considered too large and too slow in the ring.

The bulls, for the most part, were extremely large and powerful, often tossing not only the dogs but their owners many feet in the air. Men would race across the ring to catch the falling dogs on their shoulders, in their arms, or with outstretched aprons.

A writer described such a contest in 1598:

> They are fastened behind, and then worried by great English Bulldogs, but not without great risk to the dogs, from the horns of one and the teeth of the other, and it sometimes happens that they are killed on the spot; but fresh ones are immediately supplied in the places of those winded or tired. To the entertainment there often follows that of whipping a blinded bear.

In 1800 Sir William Pulteney MP introduced a Bill to ban bull-baiting with dogs. During fierce debate, future Prime Minister George Canning

Westminster Pit.

declared that 'the amusement inspired courage and produced a nobleness of sentiment and elevation of mind.' The Bill was lost by only two votes which prompted *The Times* newspaper to approvingly state that any law which interfered with how a man chose to spend his leisure was tyranny.

The sport was finally made illegal in 1835, at the same time as bear-baiting. Dog-fighting, which had also become widespread, took its place and was centred mainly at Westminster Pit in London. At this time, terrier blood was being crossed with that of the Bulldog to enhance the dog's agility.

This sport in turn became illegal, and many of the top breeders gave up. The battle may have been over but the Bulldog had a lot to live down. Respectable people associated him with rogues and vagabonds, and the dog's friends were, in the main, low-life frequenters of taverns, brothels and other disreputable haunts.

Bear-Baiting

Bear-baiting was probably the most popular of all baiting sports in its heyday and, because of its sheer expense, sponsored mainly by the Crown or the courts of wealthy noblemen. To organize the events, 'bear wards' were appointed, and these were considered to be important court officials.

Bear-baiting was conducted in a similar way to bull-baiting: the bear was chained to a stake in a pit or 'garden' designed for the purpose, and the dogs sent in to attack it. Frequently the bear was blinded before the contest. The bear that survived the ordeal was most unfortunate, for his replacement value was such that he would usually be kept to fight another day.

Sir Walter Raleigh compared the London Bear Gardens with Westminster Abbey as an important sight for visiting foreign dignitaries. When the Spanish Ambassador visited England in 1623 he was delighted by his visit to the Paris Gardens, 'where they showed him all the pleasures they could both with bull, horse, and bear, besides jackasses and apes. They turned a white bear into the Thames where the dogs baited him while swimming, which was the best sport of all.'

Bear-baiting largely died out in the eighteenth century, partly because it had become so expensive to import bears – which had long been extinct in Britain and were becoming extremely rare in Europe. It was formally outlawed in 1835 (along with bull-baiting), thanks to a Bill introduced by South Durham MP Joseph Pease who was a member of the RSPCA committee.

Badger-Baiting

Frequent badger-baits and cock-fights took place at the notorious Axbridge Square. Badgers were placed in boxes and the dogs were then expected to draw, drag or worry them out of their shelter. A badger could make a formidable opponent, with its razor-sharp claws, teeth and jaws. A variation of this sport was known as 'turn loose'. A strong piece of string was tied to the badger's tail and then fastened to a ring on the floor. The badger could then attack and retreat in and out of the box provided for this purpose.

Badger-baiting has long since been illegal, but the sport continues today, although Bulldogs are not used.

Ratting

Here the dog is expected to kill a given number of rats within a set period of time. The most celebrated of these rat killers was a Bulldog-terrier cross named Billy, who weighed 27 pounds (12.2kg). Billy's best record was to kill one hundred rats in five and a half minutes; and by 1825, it was claimed that he had destroyed 4,000 rats in as little as seventeen hours. On 13 May 1821, the owner of the rat-pit wagered a silver collar that Billy could finish off one hundred rats in twelve minutes; in fact it took him just eleven.

Salvation

In 1859 began the dawning of a new era and the salvation of what was by now a defunct and splintered breed: this was the advent of the dog show.

Many famous dogs came to the fore during this period, such as King Dick, Old King Cole, Monarch, Donald, Thunder, Crib, Diogenes, Sancho Panza, Sir Anthony, and Brutus. James Hinks is considered to be the first Bulldog exhibitor (1860–1864). The show was held at Birmingham Agricultural Hall, drew an entry of forty Bulldogs, among which was the celebrated, red, forty-pound (18kg) dog, King Dick, owned by Jacob Lamphier who was responsible for drawing up the first standard description of the Bulldog.

King Dick was not only the first Bulldog to attain the title of Champion, but the first to be registered in the Kennel Club *Stud Book* (number 2633). It was claimed that his strain could be traced back over one

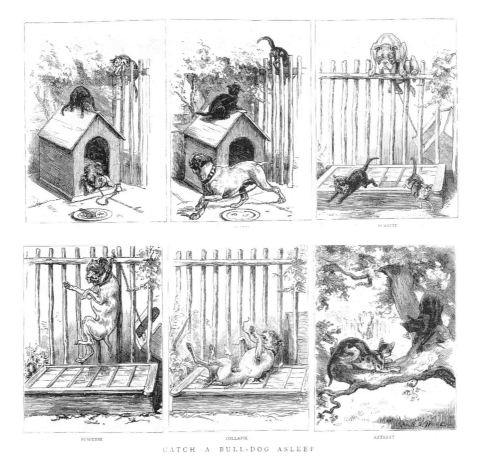

CATCH A BULL-DOG ASLEEP

'Catch a Bull-Dog Asleep': Victorian print.

hundred years. He was whelped in 1858 and died in 1866; and he was sired by Tommy out of a bitch named Slut! It is said that when Mr Lamphier contracted Tuberculosis, King Dick never left his side and, when his master died, he refused all food and passed away four days later.

By this time many breeders were carefully introducing Pug crosses to the breed, and these are generally accepted as having been a strong force in contributing to the present-day facial conformation of the Bulldog, as well as to his amiable temperament. Pugs had been imported from China in the sixteenth century by the Portuguese, and their progeny had been freely crossed with Alaunt and Mastiff crosses.

King Dick was generally accepted by the public of the time to be the first dog to display these greatly changed characteristics. King Dick's mantle passed to Crib, a brindle-and-white dog sixty-four pounds (29kg) in weight and regarded in his day as the best ever! (John Scott's engraving of Crib shows that the distinctive features of the Bulldog were already quite definite by this period.) Although Crib was considered a heavyweight, he was of the extraordinarily active type that flourished in the 1860s and 1870s, when it was fashionable to combine in the breed the ability to tackle a bull as well as keep pace with a dog-cart for hours on end. Crib was considered to possess almost 100 per cent of the show points that could possibly be found in a single dog, falling short of perfection with his front teeth, which were slightly out of alignment, and his eyes, which showed a miniscule departure from the perfect shape.

Many prominent breeders during this period, namely Mr S.E. Shirley, Mr G. Roper, and the well-known Welsh squire Mr R.J. Lloyd Price strove not so much to secure size but to follow the standards set down by Mr Lamphier. Mr Lloyd Price purchased two of King Dick's progeny, Romanie and Madge, from Mr Lamphier, paying the unheard of sum of £200.00. Romanie showed with distinction at the Birmingham show of 1865, but was later found suffocated in the guard's van of the train. The railway company offered £2.00 in compensation. Mr Lloyd Price later reminisced, 'I had him stuffed, curled up on a stool, and there he is still, a warning against the investment of too great sums in livestock.'

Mr Price was to suffer another unfortunate indignity. His Bulldog, Michael the Archangel, so named because of his most angelic smile, was sold after a tempting offer was received from France. However, Michael was not, alas, destined for further fame, for he arrived in France just months before the infamous siege of Paris during which he landed up in the stewpot along with the rest of the city's animals.

From the 1860s to the 1880s, many other dogs came to the fore. Mr Jesse Oswell's Dan, Mr Clement Butler's Stead, Mr Henshaw's Duke and Juno, Mr Verrinder's Poll, and Mr Dawes's Maggie Lauder. There were few if any affixes in those days, and for the industrious enthusiasts compiling a volume of Bulldog pedigrees containing no fewer than 6,000 animals, this was unfortunate. Mr Rawdon Lee recalls finding as many as sixty-five pedigree Bulldogs bearing the name Crib and a further thirty dogs called Duke!

The Bulldog of the 1880s had become a somewhat lighter version of famous dogs of the previous decade, and many breeders looked for a means of producing heavier specimens. A well-known and knowledgeable breeder, Mr D. Adcock, imported a huge Spanish dog named Toro, weighing in at over ninety pounds (41kg). However, as a stud force, Toro proved to be something of a disappointment: he did not live up to the initial promise that he was widely considered to possess and that was discussed in a piece about him published in *The Field* in 1871.

> … a massive dark-chestnut or carroty or brindled dog with blackish muzzle; he has very deep flews, high temples, large nostrils, and he is very much underhung, and, for his size, short in the face. His eyes are tolerably full, and a good deal of white is shown; the 'stop', or indentation between the eyes, is large and deep, and runs high up the head. The skin about the head is very loose, and falls into wrinkles and folds when the ears of the dog are erected; and a deep double dewlap runs from the angles of the mouth to the sternum. His ears have been cut out, very little of the burr being left, and this greatly detracts from the size of the head. …
>
> Toro, although very forbidding in appearance is exceedingly quiet and docile, and is possessed of great intelligence; he retains all the peculiar attributes of the ancient British Bulldog – such as size and courage. He will pin an animal only by the head and when fighting is perfectly silent and utterly regardless of pain. He is rather slow in his movements, has a rolling kind of gait, and carries his head low.

Although bull- and bear-baiting had been made illegal, the Bulldog's capacity for it, encapsulated in his size, strength and courage, continued to be of importance to the breed's enthusiasts. In this latter half of the nineteenth century, references continued to be made to the Bulldog's grit and utter indifference to physical pain. It was well known that they seldom if ever barked, and the famous dog writer, 'Stonehenge', observed that 'as the Bulldog are nearly silent, their bite is far worse than their bark'. Many people believed the Bulldog's brain to be proportionately smaller than other breeds', and that this accounted for his brute courage, tenacity, and total disregard of pain. Stonehenge went on to say,

> First they always make their attack at the head; and secondly, they do not bite and let go their hold, but retain it in the most tenacious manner, so that they can with difficulty be removed by any force that can be applied. Instances were recorded in which Bulldogs have hung on to the lip of the bull after their entrails had been torn out, and while they were in the last agonies of death.

The First Standard

Jacob Lamphier is credited with drawing up the first standard description of the Bulldog in 1864, although it was not published until 1879 when it appeared in Vero Shaw's *The Illustrated Book of the Dog* (Cassell, London):

1. **The Ears**. (1) Size: should be small. (2) Thinness. (3) Situation: they should be on the top of the head. (4) Carriage: They should be either 'rose', 'button' or 'tulip' ears. The 'rose' ear folds at the back: the top laps over outwards, exposing part of the inside. The 'button' ear only differs from the 'rose' in the falling of the tip, which laps over in front, hiding the interior completely. The 'tulip' ear is nearly erect: it is the least desirable form.
2. **The Skull**. (exclusive of property no. 4). (1) Size: should be large. (2) Height: this should be great. (3) Prominence of the cheeks: they should extend well beyond the eyes. (4) Shortness (i.e., breadth in comparison to length). (5) Shape of forehead: it should be well wrinkled and not prominent, as in the King Charles spaniel.
3. **The Eyes**. (1) Colour: should be as black as possible. (2) Shape of the opening of the lids: should be quite round. (3) Size: should be moderate. (4) Position: they should be quite in front of the head, as far from the ear and as near to the nose as possible – very far apart, but not so far as to interfere with point 3 of the second property, and neither prominent nor deeply set in the head. (5) Direction of the corners: they should be at right angles to a line drawn down the centre of the face.
4. **The Stop**. (this is an indentation between the eyes). (1) Depth. (2) Breadth. (3) Length: it should extend some considerable distance up the head.
5. **The Face**. (1) Shortness, measured from the front of the cheek bone to the end of the nose: this point cannot be carried in too great an excess. (2) Wrinkles: these should be deep and close together. (3) Shape: the muzzle should turn upwards.

In November 1908 J. Hay Hutchinson published *The Perfect Bulldog* (Bulldog Club Inc., 1903), which explained the Standard with text and accompanying illustrations. It was reprinted by the club in 1977 as a service to Bulldog lovers worldwide. On the final page there is an interesting chart of the 100 points used to judge the breed, and the relative value of the properties mentioned in the foregoing Standard:

MOUTH:	Width and squareness of jaw	2
	Projection and upward turn of lower jaw	2
	Size and condition of teeth	1
		5
CHOP:	Breadth	2
	Depth	2

	Complete covering of front teeth	1
		5
FACE:	Shortness	1
	Breadth	1
	Depth	1
	Shape and upward turn of muzzle	1
	Wrinkles	1
		5
STOP:	Depth	2
	Breadth	2
	Extent	1
		5
SKULL:	Size	5
	Height	1
	Breadth and squareness	3
	Shape	2
	Wrinkles	4
		15
EYES:	Position	2
	Size	1
	Shape	1
	Colour	1
		5
EARS:	Position	1
	Shape	1½
	Size	1½
	Thinness	1
		5
CHEST AND NECK:	Length	1
	Thickness	1
	Arch	1
	Dewlap	1
	Width, depth and roundness of chest	1
		5

SHOULDERS:	Size	2
	Breadth	2
	Muscle	1
		5

BODY:	Depth and thickness of brisket	2
	Capacity and roundness of ribs	3
		5

BACK ROACH:	Shortness	2
	Width of shoulders	1
	Shape, strength and arch at loin	2
		5

FORELEGS:	Stoutness	1½
	Shortness	1
	Development	1
	Feet	1½
		5

HIND LEGS:	Stoutness	1
	Length	1
	Shape and development	2
	Feet	1
		5

SIZE		5
COAT		5
TAIL		5
GENERAL APPEARANCE		10

100

(Reproduced by kind permission of The Bulldog Club Incorporated)

Early Shows

Once entered, dogs were expected to attend each day of the show; as a result, many were left on the benches overnight to avoid paying costly removal fees. Companies were employed by the show organizers, at no expense to the exhibitors, to feed and water the dogs, and also to

22

Five show Bulldogs from the late Victorian era: (top left) Mr F. W. Crowther's Enfield Tartlet; (top right) Mr R. D. Thomas's Bull bitch, Bicester Beauty; (bottom left) The Bull bitch, Breda, and the Bull dog Champion Forceps, owned by the famous Sam Woodiwiss; (bottom right) the Bull bitch Champion Cigarette, property of Edgar Farman, author of The Bulldog: a Monograph. *(Reproduced courtesy of The Bulldog Club Inc.)*

'Notes at the Bull Dog Show', December 1883.

Three show dogs from the turn of the century: Ch. Nuthurst Doctor (born 1901), owned by Mrs Edgar Waterlow (left).

sawdust and disinfect the floors.

Judging to the Standard also involved the complicated use of a scale of points. This system was extremely long and drawn out, and some shows might last four days. A show held in 1883 drew a fine entry of 123 dogs and, being judged on a points system, lasted a mammoth six days.

By the late 1880s, matches between two dogs were becoming common – almost a craze with wagers of £5.00 to £50.00 (huge sums in those days) being made on a single dog. Even puppies would draw large bets in matches between exhibits as young as eight weeks old. And the size of the bets was such that the wagering was reminiscent of what had taken place at the bull- and bear-baiting contests of previous years.

Turn of the Century

By the close of the nineteenth century very few breeders bred for fighting. The vast majority of dogs were bred with exhibitions and showing in mind. Many large kennels sprang up, both here and in the United States, with prominent breeders

Bulldog bred by Mrs Buichler of Guernsey in 1910. Weight 50lb.

Champion Leone Hazelwyn, 'Queen of Show bench', 1911. (Reproduced courtesy of The Bulldog Club Inc.)

such as Robert Hartley, Charles Hopton (Rodney affix.) and Walter Jeffries (Stone). Dogs were exported back and forth over the Atlantic. One such, Jeffries's dog Rodney Stone, was sold to a Mr Richard Croker Jnr for the enormous sum of $5,000.

One of Bulldogdom's greatest names during the late 1890s was Sam Woodiwiss, a breeder who had four homebred champions in his kennel at one time: Ch. Boaz, Ch. Baron Sedgemere, Ch. Battledora, and Ch. Blackberry. Mr Woodiwiss paid what was then a record sum of $250 for Dockleaf, a dog that had never been entered in a show! He was shown in 1892, and fortunately he proved to be not only a consistent winner but a prolific sire.

Toy Bulldogs

At the early shows, Bulldogs' weight varied from year to year, according to the fashion of the moment, and so classifications for Bulldogs over and under eighteen pounds (8.2kg) were introduced. Classes for the smaller animals were well filled, and these dogs became known as Toy Bulldogs, although the name was later changed to Miniature Bulldog. They were exactly as their name describes – a Bulldog in miniature – although quite often their ears were not of the small, neat, rose type, but rather a 'bat ear' like the French Bulldog's. (Indeed, many of these dogs found their way to France with the emigrating Nottingham lacemakers, where they may possibly have helped to lay the foundations for the French breed.)

The Miniature Bulldog enjoyed only a short career. It had Challenge Certificate status from 1896 to 1914 and, during this time, twenty champions were made up. The breed did not survive the First World War. Lady Kathleen Pilkington's Ch. Chevet Punch was one of the last champions, being made up in 1911 and winning the Crufts CC that same year.

Two show dogs from the 1930s: Muiravon-side Rodney (born 26 February 1932), owned by H. Riley, Godley Kennels, Hyde. (Photo: The Bulldog Club Inc.)

The Wars

At the outbreak of the First World War, Bulldog registrations were in excess of 1,500 per year with an estimated 12,000 dogs in the United Kingdom. All wars, with their ensuing manpower and food scarcities, have a devastating effect on dogdom. Breeders had to prune back harshly, and as a result many dogs were destroyed. Maintaining the best stock was achieved only by sacrifices on the part of the owners. For the duration of the war it was necessary to obtain licences to breed litters and, as these were virtually impossible to obtain, registrations dropped by over 50 per cent in the first three years.

Up until the Second World War, the breed had managed a steady recovery, with 1,000 registrations a year and an estimated 8,000 Bulldogs in the UK, but by 1945 this number had dropped by 58 per cent. The lowest ebb came in 1941 when registrations plummeted to an all-time low of just 270. However, seven years later in 1948, an overwhelming surge of national optimism resulted in 2,441 registrations – the highest ever recorded.

Throughout wartime, almost all shows ceased: only members'

Ch. Hollycroft Sugar, 1930. (Photo: The Bulldog Club Inc.)

Bulldogs used to promote the war effort.

shows were permitted, and these could be attended only by exhibitors living within a twenty-mile radius of it since there was no petrol available for private use. Shows were resumed in 1946, the first being staged by The London Bulldog Society. Dogs were judged by Frank Walker of the well-known 'Newington' prefix, bitches by Mrs E.E. Smith of the celebrated Leodride kennel.

Ch. Broadford Joan (1950s). (Photo: The Bulldog Club Inc.)

27

Ch. Cannerton Rougle (1950s) owned by Mrs Ena Parker, and sired by Milord of the Regions. (Photo: The Bulldog Club Inc.)

Personalities and Well-Known Kennels

The number of famous names and prolific kennels that existed between the wars could fill more than one book on their own. Mr Carlo Clark's Mersstham kennel was known to house over one hundred Bulldogs in its heyday. The Pearson's Westalls kennel produced several champions of note, and Mrs Pearson made breed history by becoming the first lady president of the Bulldog Club incorporated in 1936.

Mrs Ivy Palmer was known for her large kennel of Cloverleys Bulldogs at Putney, and the Naylor brothers were renowned for their Ch. Dunscar Draftsman. In the early 1920s this dog held the record for siring the most champions (eleven at that time). Mr Bill Edwards and his wife, of the renowned Maelor affix bred three champions in their first litter after the First World War: Ch. Maelor Uplifter, Ch. Maelor Solarium and Ch. Beautiful Bunty. The couple were known to be very attached to their dogs, and so they seldom bred a litter unless they either had the room to keep them all or, less often, could sell them to close friends.

At this time, Ernest Roddy bought a bitch called Anfield Olive. He was her third owner, and she was to produce three champions for him in the same litter: Ch. Basford Elite, Ch. Basford Ideal and Ch. Basford Gem. Between the wars, Mr Roddy owned and made up more champions than any other person in the breed at that time. He campaigned twenty-three dogs to their titles, eight of which were homebred. Ten of these twenty-three became tri-international champions.

In December 1944, a Mrs Green created a record by breeding four champions in a single litter: Ch. Easter Sensation of Wiggin, Ch. Rhydian Randy, Ch. British Barrister, and Ch. Winston Rose of Wiggin.

Other kennels of this era included the Woollon's of York affix, famous for Ch. Roseville Blaze, and Jack Barnard's equally famous

Keysoe affix. His dog, Ch. Keysoe Golden Sovereign, was campaigned at the same time as Pugilist and received ten Reserve CCs to him before attaining the all-important third CC.

One of posterity's great personalities was a bookmaker named Jimmy Knode, who purchased a red champion bitch called Bosworth Queen from her breeder, a Mr Duncan, for £200. Queenie, as she was known, rapidly took over his life and was often to be seen decked in real diamond collars. Jimmy would hire a prop plane and fly over championship shows trailing banners saying 'Queenie is here!' In 1939, Jimmy placed six pictures of his beloved bitch in a Christmas annual, one of which depicted himself and Queenie astride the globe and, underneath, his motto, 'Everyone knows Jimmy Knode never owes, pays like lightning, and always wears a rose.' All of which was true. The pair put in a major contribution to the war effort in raising over £100,000: Queenie was displayed in Trafalgar Square, London, flanked by collecting boxes, and the crowds trailed past, patting and stroking her head until she was totally bald!

Some famous stud-dogs made their mark on the breed during the Second World War, namely Ch. Maelor Solarium, Ch. Dunscar Draftsman and John Barnard's Ch. Prince of Woodgate, all of which sired eleven British champions.

John and Marjorie Barnard, who registered their Noways affix in 1932, have the distinction of having bred Ch. Noways Chuckles, the only Bulldog ever to win Supreme Champion at Crufts in 1952. Chuckles was one

Ernie Roddy of the famous Basford Kennel judging a summer championship show. His CC winners are Ch. Noways Timber, handled by Hope Barnard, and Ch. Alabama, handled by Arthur Westlake. (Photo: The Bulldog Club Inc.)

29

of three champions born in one litter; the other two were Ch. Noways Cherry and Ch. Noways Timber. Marjorie is also the only woman to have been elected as life president of the Bulldog Club Inc., a post she actively held until her death.

Jack and Kathleen Cook of the renowned Jackath affix once held the record for breeding the most homebred United Kingdom Bulldog champions. Both were well-known championship show judges, and for many years Jack was the breed correspondent for *Dog World*. In 1947 Kath won her first CC with the homebred dog Jackath Amber King. His litter-brother was sold on to the United States, where he soon became Am. Ch. Morovian He's a Mainstay. Although Jack had won his first ticket back in 1949 it was not until Bath in 1966 that he awarded Challenge Certificates for the first time. Both Jack and Kath were tremendous characters and were a familiar sight at championship shows, both as exhibitors and spectators, until they were well into their eighties. The pair would sit at the ringside and whisper comments to each other about the exhibits and their handlers. Unfortunately, these lacked volume control and their voices could have guided a tanker through Suez in the thickest of fogs.

When George and Eva Parker of Wolverhampton in the Midlands purchased their first bitch, Whitmore Beauty, it was to be the start of their

famous of the Regions line, which over the decades gave them such well-known champions as M'Lord of the Regions, Cannington Rogie of the Regions, Soldier Boy of the Regions, Waggy of the Regions, Brenuth Barrow of the Regions, Brumigum Stroller Boy of the Regions, Dough Boy of the Regions, and Archie of the Regions.

One of the breed's most memorable characters was without doubt Arthur Westlake of Teignmouth, Devon. His Baytor affix (Torbay spelt backwards) graced

Ch. Bellum Premiere, winner of the first Bulldog of the Year (1977), with judges Claude Bannister, Marjorie Barnard and Arthur Westlake. Handled by owner John Driver. (Photo: The Bulldog Club Inc.)

Ch. Thydeal Little Audie winning her seventh CC and Best of Breed at Bournemouth 1966, and handled by the late Audie Hayball and judge Anita Westlake. (Photo: The Bulldog Club Inc.)

many champions, such as Merrymaker, Greathill Bunty, Bosun, Enterprise, Telstar, Zircon Solo, and Holeyn Hell of a Fella. Arthur's partner and future wife Miss Anita Woodthorpe was very instrumental in the success of this kennel. Although nowadays better known for her great success in Chows, Anita is still a respected championship show judge of Bulldogs and has judged the breed at Crufts on two occasions. When Arthur judged, his expression said it all: if the dog was wry he would twist his mouth; if it was unsound he would shuffle; if it was 'pet quality' he would stand and scratch his head; and if it was a stunner his face would beam. For many years Arthur was president of the British Bulldog Club and was also very involved with general committee work at the Kennel Club. The breed's greatest champion died in 1980.

Harold and Audie Hayball's Thydeal kennel started in the early 1960s. They sprang to fame with their homebred multiple-CC-winning bitch Ch. Thydeal Little Audie, who was followed by Ch. Thydeal Relentless, Ch. Thydeal Easter Piece, Ch. Thydeal Golden Wonder and, in more recent times, Ch. Thydeal Gentle Breeze. A knowledgeable Bulldogger, Harold in latter years was honoured with the presidency of the Italian Bulldog Club, a position he held until his death in 1997.

Another keenly interested couple were Ralph and Margaret Chambers, whose Castizo affix was carried by such dogs as Ch. Castizo Drummond, Ch. Castizo Hamish and the famous Ch. Castizo Canford Trailblazor, sire of Ch. Denbrough Leander. Since Ralph passed away Margaret has continued to be active as a knowledgeable Bulldog judge.

Les Lund started his Qualco kennel back in the 1950s and has produced such championships as the Int. Ch. Qualco Marksman and

Ch. Aldridge Apalation handled by Les Cotton. Ellen and Les Cotton's Aldridge kennel have consistently bred top-winning show stock for decades. (Photo: Simon Lathan.)

Ch. Qualco Weavervale Brandy, owned by Geoff Nichols. Both Geoff and Les are well-known judges, Geoff having officiated at the World Show. Les maintains a keen interest in the breed but is nowadays better known as secretary of Manchester Championship Dog Show.

Claude Bannister of the Thatchway kennel will always be remembered as the perfect English gentleman. Always a champion of the breed's interests, he was President of the British Bulldog Club until his death.

Les and Ellen Cotton's Aldridge kennel has been one of the most consistent, producing a strong, distinct, easily recognizable type. Stars have included the legendary Ch. Aldridge Anemone and Ch Aldridge Advent Gold, sire of nine UK champions. Other champions have included Ch. Aldridge Avanti, sire of four UK champions and Ch. Aldridge Aristocrat of Brandywell, sire of five UK champions and, more recently, Ch. Aldridge Apalation. The couple are both international championship show judges, and their lines can be traced back in almost all of today's show stock.

Norman and Ada Pitts of the Allomdom affix are stalwarts of the breed, and the couple hold the distinction of owning the only Bulldog to win Best of Breed at Crufts on three occasions. Walvra Red Ensign was followed by Ch. Allomdom Dilkusha Crusader and Ch. Allomdom Encounter. Norman is president of the Bulldog Club Incorporated. This dedicated couple have worked ceaselessly for the good and wellbeing of the breed; both are highly respected championship show judges, and both have judged the breed at Crufts.

Billy and Margaret Goodwin's Britishpride kennel has for many years consistently produced winning stock, most notable of which are Ch. Britishpride Hanky Panky, Ch. Petworth Passion Potter of Britishpride, and Ch. Ocobo Royal Heritage of Britishpride who went Best in Show at the British Bulldog Club Centenary Show and gained his title at Crufts. The Goodwins have made Bulldog showing a family affair: their son and two daughters are a familiar sight around the ringside.

The Ocobo kennel of Pat and Norman Davis produced countless champions, among these the famous sire Ch. Ocobo Skipper. Others of note include Ch. Storming Passion of Ocobo, bred by Mrs Rich and winner of Bulldog of the Year in 1989. Pat, an international championship show judge, has continued under the affix to produce one of the top winning dogs of the decade, Ch. Ocobo Tully. Pat's son Kevin has carried on the family tradition: he has enjoyed marked success with his own Mystyle kennel, and he is also a championship show judge. Norman also continues with the affix as Ocobo Bronorn in partnership with Vicky Roach. The couple have campaigned Ch. Shebador Our Floyd and Ch. Shebador Katie Fair and Ch. Bronorn Surrealist to their titles, and have more recently made up their homebred dog Ch. Ocobo Just Do It Bronorn.

Gwen and the late Stan Biddle of the Gwenstan affix were ardent campaigners throughout the 1980s when the couple produced the champion bitch Gwenstan Lady Le Turves. In recent years Gwen has been much in demand both here and overseas as a respected championship show judge.

The Hobtop kennel's Jean and Peter Booth have been keen supporters of the northern clubs for countless years and have built a reputation for their own well-balanced definite type. Peter is a forthright Yorkshireman, and both he and Jean's views are always in demand in their capacity as judges both in the UK and overseas. The couple, whose champion bitch Snow Queen was Crufts CC winner, have produced dogs such as the beautiful Hobtop Charisma and Ch. Hobtop Sentinel; and more recently they have enjoyed success with the lovely bitch Ch. Eliza Doolittle of Hobtop.

One of my favourite bitches, Ch. Eliza Doolittle of Hobtop, handled by her owner Jean Booth. (Photo: Simon Lathan.)

Bill and Sheila Roberts purchased their first Bulldog in 1978 and started breeding and showing under their Isgraig affix in 1980. Their first champion, Isgraig Looby Lou, followed the next year, and she produced the legendary Ch. Isgraig Red Baron, sire of nine UK champions including their top-winning bitch Ch. Isgraig Bella Vega. I remember being very impressed with their strong-headed brindle boy, Isgraig Horatio, litterbrother to Red Baron. The couple are respected and knowledgeable championship judges, much in demand both in the UK and overseas.

Pat Dellar and her Merriveen kennel have without doubt been the biggest influence on the breed since the 1970s. I have always enjoyed her company and agreed with her often forthright views. For many years, Pat had been a most successful breeder of Boxers such as the celebrated Ch. Fascination and the Supreme Champion Hazelnut, who could trace his pedigree back to a Merriveen Poodle.

When I entered the breed, Pat's dogs seemed to be not only cosmetically appealing, but better balanced than most, and I knew instantly that this was the type that I liked. My first star Jacob was sired by Pat's famous and prolific stud-dog Ch. Merriveen Happy Daze, the sire of seven UK champions; and all my resulting stock has always been prodigiously bred back to either Jacob or similar Merriveen lines. Other notable dogs from this kennel include Ch. Merriveen Halcyon Daze, sire of five UK champions, Ch. Merriveen Pepsi Cola, Ch. Merriveen Tipsi Cola, and Merriveen Son of Satan, producer of six UK champions. This kennel has bred twelve UK champions, a record for the breed.

Dora and the late George Wakefield are probably amongst the most well known of all Bulldoggers worldwide. George was a great character with his trademark deerstalker hat, a tradition carried on by his son-in-law, Brian Daws. The most famous dogs from this Outdoors kennel must be Ch. Outdoors Jubilant and his son Ch. Outdoors Jubi Junior, one of my all-time favourites and the winner of twenty-four Challenge Certificates. Jubilant was Pup of the Year in 1978, winning his title at the age of one year and one week. Jubi Junior made his title in one year and one day. Daughter Judith has been a successful breeder and exhibitor of Bichon Frise under her Daisybank affix, and with Brian has campaigned such dogs as Ch. Outdoors Country Gent, Bulldog of the Year in 1995, and Ch. Kentee Kizzy of Outdoors.

Chris Thomas of the Kingrock kennel entered the breed as a result of attending the Bulldog Club Incorporated Centenary Show in 1975. He purchased his first Bulldog, Chiansline White Regality, from John and Sheila Alcock, and by 1979 he had produced his first champion, Merriveen

Two of the breed's most respected stalwarts, Norman and Ada Pitts. The occasion is The Italian Bulldog Club Speciality Championship Show, and the Best in Show exhibit is Ch. King Lion di Hawkroad, handled by his breeder, Paola Bonnetto.

Maybe Baby. Soon afterwards he made up the litter-brother, Ch. Kingrock Captain Christian. These were followed by Ch. Kingrock Freezo, Ch. Kingrock Canis Pugnax and his son Int. Nord. & UK Ch. Kingrock Buster. In the late 1980s I introduced Chris to Graham Godfrey, and the partnership have gone on to make up dogs such as Ch. Amurton Dirty Harry of Kingrock, and the Crufts 1993 Best of Breed winner Ch. Tretun Sam Wella of Kingrock.

Les and Dorrie Thorpe have owned Bulldogs since 1952, and both are championship judges. They have made up nine homebred champions, the first of which was Tuffnuts First Lady. Les has worked ceaselessly for many years as secretary of the British Bulldog Club and is to judge the breed at Crufts in the year 2000.

Some people experience a run of bad luck in the breed, and it is only their determination that wins through in the end. Anne and Fred Higginbottom are such a couple. They have spent almost forty years in the breed, having founded their Tretun kennel with Canford Boadicea. Their first champion, Aldridge Aphrodite was made up in 1973 but then died of cancer in 1974. In 1979 they produced Tretun Mr Jingle who gained two CCs before dying tragically of thrombosis. A new bitch, Worston Little Lady of Tretun proved to be the start of seventeen exciting years, for she produced the kennel's first homebred champion, Ch. Tretun Mr Bumble and Int. Ch. Tretun Barnaby Rudge. These were followed by Ch. Tretun Imogen at Rockytop, Ch. Tretun Sam Wella at Kingrock, Int. Ch. Tretun Buster Sam at Kingrock, and Ch. Tretun Mr Barkiss. Their most noted champion was Ch. Tretun Matilda, Top Bulldog in 1990 and 1991. Both Anne and Fred are championship show judges and have officiated all over the world. Anne judged Crufts in 1993, and has for the last twenty years been secretary of the Sheffield and District Bulldog Club.

Ch. Tretun Miss Matilda flying the flag. Matilda, owned and bred by Anne and Fred Higginbottom, was Top Bulldog in 1991 and 1992. She won 17 Challenge Certificates and was often used as the mascot for international sporting events.

Doug and Anne Heeley established their Wedgebury affix in 1967, and they are both championship judges. Ch. Wedgebury Miss Biddy was followed by Wedgebury Warlord who sired Ch. Merriveen Pepsi Cola and Ch. Thydeal Sweet Sherry. Overseas champions have included Ch. Wedgebury Wizard and Ch. Wedgebury War Bonnet.

Carol Newman's parents were already in Bulldogs some thirty years ago with their affix Wencar (derived by combining the names of Carol and her sister Wendy). Much experience and knowledge was gained by Carol's association with Jack and Kath Cook (Jackath), and Carol has successfully reared over fifty litters.

Carol has bred ten overseas champions and campaigned the following Bulldogs to their titles: Ch. Jackath Silver Moonlight, Ch. Jackath Casandra of Vondallaans, Ch. Jackath Glint of Gold, Ch. Jackath Solo, Ch. Wencar Silver Sheen, Ch. Esclusham Song of Sixpence, and Ch. Esclusham Golden Chimes of Wencar. She has judged throughout the world at championship level since 1979.

The Wildax kennel has bred notable Bulldogs such as Ch. Wildax Fancy Nancy and the 1994 Crufts Best of Breed winner Wildax Paris. The Wildax affix has also graced many champions in other breeds (Ch. Wildax

Bruce Tuttle handling his homebred Ch. Bowlaine Fine Harvest. (Photo: Simon Lathan.)

Lovelace is the Boston Terrier breed-record holder). A family-run kennel, it is also well known for its championship Boxers. Margaret, Frank and daughter Ann are all championship show judges.

Other kennels of note include John and the late Sheila Nattrass's Bonifacio, Brian and Mary Taylor's Bramor Dawn Mantle and Phil Green's Dawnstars, Bruce Tuttle's the Bowlaine, Pauline Horner's Honclo, Jim Adam's Leydud, Fred and Margaret Haynes Marlil, Jackie and Vic Haynes's Barranco, Marguerite and George Cook's Eskaidee, and Pat Perkins's Quintic.

Ruth Murray's Brenuth Bulldogs have been consistent winners throughout the decades, as have the dogs of Frank Huxley's Ellesmere affix. Despite serious debilitating illness, Paul and Rosemarie Kent (Hyten) have consistently bred quality litters, and Maureen Mortham's Packapunch affix has graced several overseas champions as well as Our Boy Max, a Best of Breed winner at Crufts (1989). The Berrybrook kennel of Chris and Sally Carberry have produced such winning stock as Ch. Berrybrook Born to Boogie and Ch. Berrybrook Buttons and Bows, while the Rodger and Fletcher partnership's Belushi kennel continues to breed CC-winning stock such as Ch. Belushi Floy Joy. There is also the famous Dewrie kennel of John and Eirwen Davies in Wales, and the Brampton affix of Terry and Angela Davison is flying the flag in the United States, where Brampton Jay Junior is making an impact.

The New Enthusiasts

The breed is indeed fortunate to have such an influx of new keen blood.

Slow and steady is the name of the game in Bulldogs, although many have achieved remarkable success in their breeding programmes in a relatively short space of time. These include Brenda Price whose Esclusham kennel finished Top Breeders in 1997, the Cavills whose lovely bitch Ch. Delrousher Fantasy Delight finished Top Bulldog in 1997.

Quality stock being produced by new enthusiasts. Newrock Sophie Tucker owned and bred by Jackie and Peter New of Sunderland.

Others include Peter and Jackie New, whose Newrock affix has produced the Reserve CC winner Newrock Sophie Tucker and the S.A. Ch. Newrock Sebastian of Kelloe. Anna Williams and Dominic Lawrence have bred their first Champion, Athelston Anglorum, owned and campaigned by Chrissie Jeffreys and the Plymouth-based St Levan Kennel of Martin and Wendy Lathan is building strong foundation bloodlines. Mark Davis has bred his first homebred champion, Ch. Kilsyth Glory Lass, and Rob Harris is starting to produce a distinct type, having for several years campaigned several of the late Margaret Hazelman's Petworth stock to their titles. Mark Burridge has successfully campaigned his homebred boy Ch. Diadem Gold Bullion to his title, and Sonia Davis's team of homebred Rowendale Bulldogs are seldom out of the cards at championship shows. The Grieves and Hetherington partnership has produced the super-boned CC-winning dog Shaftcraggs White Mischief from two Kelloe dogs, and the Kofyn kennel of Malcolm Presland and Mel Vincent are enjoying success with stock from similar bloodlines. Kevin Banner and Fay Stokes have made up their first champion, Britishpride Red Lipstick at Sabany, and at the time of writing Sharon Anderson's homebred Tuffntrusty Queenie is winning CCs. Hillplace is the affix of Maria Colacicco and Ralph Taylor, who are enjoying success of late with their homebred youngster, Hillplace Ironbrew.

The Bulldog at Crufts

By the time that Charles Cruft held his first dog show, Bulldogs had been exhibited for thirty years, The Bulldog Club Incorporated had been in existence for some sixteen years, and the winners of the bitch and dog Challenge Classes were the fifty-first and fifty-second Bulldog champions to be made up.

At this time, wins in the Challenge Class were accumulated so that a dog could win his championship title (six points were needed for a dog to become a champion). Crufts was not yet one of the largest shows, so there was only one point on offer for a win there; the larger shows had two points on offer.

Crufts Stars

In 1927, Ch. Dame Daggers won the Bitch Challenge Certificate, from 1929 her daughter, Ch. Dame's Double, did a triple, winning the Bitch Challenge Certificates three years running. Dame's Double was sired by Ch. Sessue and bred by Mr A.G. Sturgeon. She held the pre-war Bitch CC record with twenty-four Challenge Certificates.

Ch. Ritestok Robinhood was Best of Breed in 1950 and 1951, the latter year with an entry of 299 Bulldogs and 119 exhibits. This was the third time ever that more than 100 Bulldogs were collected together to compete at a championship show. The judge that year was Mr E. Roddy, whose Basford dogs had won two pre-war Crufts CCs.

The only Bulldog to win Best in Show at Crufts was Marjorie Barnard's Ch. Noways Chuckles. She won the award in 1952, round about the time of The Festival of Britain. Chuckles, who won four Crufts CCs in total, was one of three champions from the litter by Ch. Prince of Woodgate out of the Reserve CC-winning Noways Victoria.

At this time there were no groups. All Best of Breed winners were paraded together, each dog walking in turn against the others in the ring. As a result the procedure took two and a half hours! When Chuckles took Best in Show, she and the Reserve (an English Setter), had to meet the same dogs from the previous day's placings. In 1953 Chuckles was Best Bitch, with Auraelean Autocrat taking Best of Breed. In 1954 Crufts was cancelled owing to an electricity strike, but

Marjorie Barnard with Ch. Noways Chuckles receiving the Supreme Champion cup, 'The Keppel Trophy' from Lady Northesk in January 1952. Chuckles was the only Bulldog to win Best in Show at Crufts. (Photo: The Bulldog Club Inc.)

in 1955 and 1956 Chuckles was again best of Breed. She went on to win a total of thirteen CCs, and was only once beaten by a dog (Best of Breed at Crufts 1953), and once by a bitch in Veteran Class.

Wallie and Vera May's Walvra affix has enjoyed much success at the show. In 1963 Ch. Walvra Cheri Gal won the bitch CC, and in 1964 Ch. Walvra Sans Souci, bred by Miss M. and Miss G. Sutton was Best of Breed. She was a granddaughter of the 1962 Best of Breed, Ch. Blockbuster Best Bitter, who traced back to Ch. Basford Revival, whose son was Best of Breed in 1937. Ch. Walvra Red Ensign, bred by the Mays and owned by Norman and Ada Pitts of the Allomdom affix, won three Crufts CCs (one of which was awarded by Marjorie Barnard): two with Best of Breed; he was Reserve in the group in 1969. Ensign was by Sagebrush Lord Nelson of Chadderton out of Walvra Heftigift. He was a grandson of Ch. Block-buster Rawburn Fleance, sire of Ch. Blockbuster Best Bitter.

Beating Red Ensign for Best of Breed in 1970 was John and Dorothy Jones's Ch. Broomwick Blythome Bumble Bee, bred by Mrs O. Overtong, who went on to take Reserve in the group. She was Best of Breed again in 1971. She was by Ch. Baron of Blythome out of Broomwick Golden Maiden, and she traced back to Leodride Ace, the sire of Sans Souci.

In 1973 and 1975 Bulldogs won the group. The two dogs responsible were also the winners of the CCs at the centenary show of the Bulldog Club Incorporated, the first breed club in the world to hold a centenary. They were the bitch, Ch. Portfield So Small, and the dog, Ch. Beechlyn Golden Nugget of Denbrough.

So Small was by the American-bred dog import Am. Can. Ch. Vardona's Frost Masterpiece, who was the son of Am. Ch. Vardona Frosty Snowman (winner of the group in 1960 at Westminster, the most prestigious show in the United States). Her dam was Zircon Red Pixie. She was bred in 1969 by her owner Mrs Sheila Goddard, and she won her first CC with Best of Breed at the Bulldog Club Show in 1970, when she was just six months old. She won four more groups, going on to Best in Show at the West of England Ladies' Kennel Society Show in April 1972.

Golden Nugget was the top-winning dog of any breed in 1974. He started his group-winning career the year before with Best in Group at the May Scottish Kennel Club; and in 1974 he won five groups, going on to Best in Show at Bath and Paignton. He was by Ch. Denborough Leander out of Beechlyn Carmen of Barabull, bred by Joe Fox in 1972, and he traced back to Ch. Prince of Woodgate, Chuckles' sire. He was owned by Barbara and Dennis Shaw.

Ch. Aldridge Anemone, owned by Les and Ellen Cotton and bred by Mrs Adams, won the Best in Group in 1978. She was by Ch. Brumigum

My first visit to Crufts. Top left, Pat Dellar and David McHale, the author and further along, Julia Easterling-Taylor. Second from the right, the well-known Italian breeder, Moreno Maltagliati. Centre, the late Bob Giles next to Susan Jay and her mother Cynthia. Bottom right, Dora Wakefield handles Ch. Outdoors Jubilant.

Stroller Boy of the Regions out of Sunset Solitaire, a daughter of the 1977 Best of Breed Ch. Aldridge Advent Gold (himself a son of Golden Nugget, who won Best in Show at Richmond in 1976. Anemone won seven groups in total, including her Crufts win, Best in Show at the British Utility Breeds Association, and Reserve Best in Show at Three Counties and Belfast in 1978.

Crufts has been a particularly lucky show for me, with Kelloe dogs taking best of Breed on three occasions. Ch. Tyegarth Jacob of Kelloe won Best of Breed twice, and on each occasion was beaten only by the eventual supreme Champion, the Miniature Poodle Ch. Grayco Hazelnut (1982), and the Airedale Ch. Livera's Christmas Carol (1986). Ch. Medbull Gold Dust over Kelloe qualified for Crufts at his first outing (Ladies' Kennel Association), and was possibly the youngest exhibit, all breeds, the day of the show when he took his first Challenge Certificate and Best of Breed under the highly respected breed specialist, Mrs Ada Pitts. In 1996, Gold Dust also won the Best Puppy (awarded at Crufts for the first time that year), and he went on to win thirteen CCs, and was Top Puppy and Top Bulldog of 1996.

Terry Brunton's Homebred Ch. Sandean Sophie's Baby, in her lifetime the Bitch Breed-Record holder, won three CCs at Crufts. She was By Ch. Ocobo Skipper out of Sandean Miss World, her dam being a

41

The Top Bulldog of 1996, Ch. Medbull Gold Dust over Kelloe, handled by the author, after being awarded the dog CC and Best of Breed at Midland Counties Ch. Show 1996. The bitch CC winner and the Top Bulldog of 1997, Ch. Delrousher Fantasy Delight, is handled by Brian Taylor. The judge is the famous all-rounder Brenda Banbury.

granddaughter of Ch. Aldridge Advent Gold and also a daughter of the group-winning Ch. Outdoors Jubi Junior.

Ch. Willsmere Solid Silver, bred by Graham and Viv Williams in 1986, won three Crufts CCs, with Best of Breed in 1988 and 1992. He won the group at Windsor in July 1988. He was by Advent Gold's son Ch. Aldridge Avanti out of Willsmere Naughty But Nice. Solid Silver went on to win Bulldog of the Year on four occasions, a record unequalled in the breed.

Clubs and Societies

The first British Bulldog club was formed in 1864 by a Mr R.S. Rockstro. A group of about thirty enthusiasts met at the inaugural meeting and the motto of 'Hold Fast' was adopted – somewhat prematurely as the new club lasted for only about three years. This small band were responsible for the compilation of what was to be referred to as the 'Philo Kuon Standard'. This was adopted as *The Standard* in 1865, although we know it had been predated by that of Jacob Lamphier.

Ten years later, on 13 April 1875, the club was re-established at a meeting held at the Blue Post Inn in London, and it is still regarded as the 'mother club': the oldest dog club in the world and older than the Kennel Club. The club subscription was set at one guinea (£1.05) and remains so to this day.

Robert Fulton, familiarly known as 'Scotch Bob', was a founder member of the club. His book *The Bulldog* is still in existence, although now it is extremely rare. Another influential member was Edgar Farman, who was elected to the club in 1888 and quickly set about gaining its incorporation. Six years later he joined the Kennel Club, and by 1896 he had become a member of its committee and honorary editor of its magazine *The Kennel Gazette*. A man of intense feelings, he wrote to the then Prince of Wales abhorring the widespread custom of ear-cropping and, with the prince's help, managed to persuade the Kennel club to abolish the practice. He also vigorously campaigned to encourage Bulldoggers to abandon the use of special harnessing equipment which they often used to help produce exaggerated fronts. In 1889 Farman published the first of three works, also entitled *The Bulldog* (Kennel Gazette, 1899), which many still consider to be the 'Bulldog bible'. He died in 1905.

One of the main reasons for the adoption of a universal Standard was the indiscriminate importation of the huge Spanish or milk-cart dogs, brought over in direct competition with the rather small animal being bred for ratting. It was evident that some form of controlling body was needed to lay down guidelines for breeding, and a Miniature Bulldog Club, whose main aim was to stop the growth in size and weight, existed from 1900 to the outbreak of the First World War.

The famous Pugilist, winner of 30 CCs and one of the Top Winning Bulldogs of all time. (Photo: The Bulldog Club Inc.)

Bruno and Jim 1915 – all dressed up and nowhere to go (Photo: courtesy of Martin and Wendy Lathan.)

The London Bulldog Society appeared in 1891, starting life as the South London Bulldog Society. The following year, 1892, the British Bulldog Club was formed with the intention of putting on shows for the benefit of fanciers in the North, Midlands and the provinces.

By 1901 there were some twenty-seven Bulldog Clubs. The main reason for the sudden proliferation of clubs was considered to be the geographical layout of the various shows and the lack of personal transport. Most dogs and their owners would have no option but to travel to and from on the new railway networks. Motor cars were non-existent in the nineteenth century and, except for those belonging to the extremely wealthy, were few and far between until well after the First World War. Another important factor, often overlooked, was the internal differences that raged within many of the clubs and caused divergence. Bad disputes between members is probably the reason for many of today's prominent Bulldog clubs.

There are twenty surviving Bulldog breed clubs, an inordinately large amount of clubs for the number of Bulldogs registered each year.

Many breeds have three or four times as many annual registrations with perhaps only three to four breed clubs, regionally or nationally. For several years now there has been talk of streamlining the breed clubs, either by mergers or closure. To my mind, for as long as there are people willing to run them, and others that are keen to remain members, I see no reason why they should not continue.

The Bulldog Breed Council

A breed council is a consultative body. It does not have any executive powers, but it is a means of passing on breed opinion to the Kennel Club. In turn, the Kennel Club will confer with a breed council on such matters as the Breed Standard, breed clubs, allocation of Challenge Certificates, and health matters.

After exploratory meetings between the breed clubs, the first Bulldog Breed Council was formed in 1967 at a meeting chaired by the late Group Captain 'Beefy' Sutton. Twenty-three clubs attended, and two delegates form each club reported back to their members. This first council lasted for eleven years before disbanding in acrimony.

In 1993, the breed clubs met at the Sky Blue Connection and decided to re-form the breed council with Robin Searle as Chairman and me as secretary, a position I held for two years.

The Bulldog Breed Council has a working party that has organized several well-attended breed seminars for novice judges. Pamphlets have been produced on the Breed Standard, whelping, and puppy rearing, all of which have been reprinted, and now they are to produce a voluntary breeder's sales contract.

The Future

The Bulldog has been under threat since its very inception, and I know of few other breeds who have, in the face of such difficulties, adapted so well to modern-day living. Over recent decades there has been concern that the Bulldog's conformation has compromised his physical soundness, but I take heart from the marked advances in general health of the breed since the mid-1970s. One no longer sees Bulldogs 'roar' at the summer shows – in many cases the breed fares better than many others in the heat – and the straight stifles and lameness, that were once regrettably common, now appear to be a thing of the past.

2

The Breed Standards

The majority of countries have based their own Breed Standard for the Bulldog on the one that was originally drawn up by the mother club – The Bulldog Incorporated – and published on 27 May 1875. However, along with the standards of many other breeds, the Kennel Club revised it in 1986. The basic idea was to explain things in plainer English. Since terms such as 'tacked on' can be confusing when translated into another language, and the original Standard's reference to Ayrshire bulls might be safely assumed to be meaningless in many parts of the world. Inevitably, perhaps, the Kennel Club's new version caused some controversy. I can understand both sides of the argument, but feel that the debate is one that might possibly be compared to that prompted by the new modern-day versions of the Bible: while we appreciate the reasons for the change, most of us still prefer the Authorized Version of King James (1604).

When the Bulldog Club of America was formed in 1890, it utilized the British Breed Standard. In 1896, it adopted a new standard, and this was revised in 1914 to declare the Dudley nose a disqualification. In 1976, the Dudley nose was redefined as a 'brown or liver-coloured nose', and in 1989 the Standard was re-formatted, with no changes in wording.

The purpose of any breed standard is to outline the physical conformation (and also the character or temperament) of a particular breed. It describes the ideal specimen of the breed, towards the attainment of which all breeders strive; and it is the template against which a show judge will compare each exhibit and select a winner. It can be understood from this that the wording of a breed standard is therefore very important. Even so, however precise the text is intended to be, it is inevitable that each individual will interpret the various points slightly differently, and this is what ultimately influences the future appearance of the breed.

In this respect, especially, it is interesting to look at the Club's 1875 Standard and compare it with both the current Kennel Club Bulldog

Standard and that of the American Kennel Club. All three standards are reproduced here.

The 1875 Breed Standard

(Reproduced by kind permission of The Bulldog Club Incorporated)

General Appearance

In forming a judgement on any specimen of the breed, the general appearance, which is the first impression a dog makes as a whole on the eye of the judge, should first be considered. Secondly should be noticed its size, shape and make, or rather its proportions in the relation they bear to each other. No point should be so much in excess of the others as to destroy the general symmetry, or make the dog appear deformed, or interfere with its powers of motion, etc. Thirdly, its style, carriage, gait, temper, and its several points should be considered separately in detail, due allowance being made for the bitch, which is not so grand or as well developed as the dog. The general appearance of the Bulldog is that of a smooth-coated, thick-set dog, rather low in stature, but broad, powerful and compact. The head strikingly massive, and large in proportion to the dog's size. The face extremely short. The muzzle very broad, blunt, and inclined upwards. The body short and well-knit; the limbs stout and muscular. The hindquarters very high and strong but rather lightly made in comparison with its heavily made foreparts. The dog should convey an impression of determination, strength and activity, similar to that suggested by the appearance of a thick-set Ayrshire bull. From its formation, the dog has a peculiar heavy and constrained gait, appearing to walk with short, quick steps on the tips of its toes, its hind feet not being lifted high, but appearing to skim the ground, and running with the right shoulder rather advanced, similar to the manner of a horse in cantering.

The Head and Skull

The skull should be very large – the larger the better – and in circumference should measure (round the front of the ears) at least the height of the dog at the shoulders. Viewed from the front it should appear very high from the corner of the lower jaw to the apex of the skull, and also very broad and square. The cheeks should be well rounded and extended

47

sideways beyond the eyes. Viewed at the side, the head should appear very high, and very very short from its back to the point of the nose. The forehead should be flat, neither prominent nor overhanging the face; the skin upon it and about the head very loose and well wrinkled. The projections of the frontal bones should be very prominent, broad, square and high, causing a deep and wide indentation between the eyes, termed the 'stop'; a furrow both broad and deep should extend up to the middle of the skull, being traceable to the apex. The face, measured from the front of the cheek bone to the nose, should be as short as possible, and its skin should be deeply and closely wrinkled. The muzzle should be short, broad, turned upwards and very deep from the corner of the eye to the corner of the mouth. The nose should be large, broad and black, and under no circumstances should be liver-coloured or brown; its top should be deeply set back, almost between the eyes. The distance form the inner corner of the eye (or from the centre of the stop between the eyes) to the extreme tip of the nose should not exceed the length from the tip of the nose to the edge of the under lip. The nostrils should be large, wide, and black, with a well-defined vertical straight line between them. The flews, called the 'chop', should be thick, broad, pendant and should join the under lip in front and quite cover the teeth. The jaws should be broad, massive and square, the lower jaw should project considerably in front of the upper, and turn up. Viewed from the front, the various properties of the face must be equally balanced on either side of an imaginary line down the centre of the face.

Eyes

The eyes seen from the front should be situated low down in the skull, as far from the ears as possible. The eyes and the 'stop' should be in the same straight line, which should be at right angles to the furrow. They should be as wide apart as possible, provided their outer corners are within the outline of the cheeks. They should be quite round in shape, of moderate size, neither sunken nor prominent, and in colour should be very dark – almost, if not quite, black, showing no white – when looking directly forward.

Ears

The ears should be set high on the head – i.e. the front inner edge of each ear should (as viewed from the front) join the outline of the skull at the top corner of such outline, so as to place them as wide apart and as high and as far from the eyes as possible. In size they should be small and thin. The shape termed as 'rose ear' is correct and folds inwards at its back, the upper or front edge curving over outwards and backwards, showing part of the inside burr.

Mouth

The jaw should be broad and square and have the six small front teeth between the canines in an even row; the canine teeth or tusks wide apart. The teeth should not be seen when the mouth is closed. The teeth should be large and strong. When viewed from the front, the under jaw should be centrally under the upper jaw to which it should also be parallel.

Neck

The neck should be moderate in length (rather short than long) very thick, deep and strong. It should be well arched at the back, with much loose, thick and wrinkled skin about the throat, forming a dewlap on each side from the lower jaw to the chest.

Forequarters

The shoulders should be broad, sloping and deep, very powerful and muscular, and giving the appearance of having been 'tacked on' to the body. The brisket should be capacious, round and very deep from the top of the shoulders to its lowest part where it joins the chest, and be well let down between the forelegs. It

should be large in diameter and round behind the forelegs (not flat sided, the ribs being well rounded). The forelegs should be very stout and strong, set wide apart, thick, muscular and straight, with well developed forearms, presenting a rather bowed outline, but the bones of the leg should be large and straight,

Ch. Petworth Pansy Potter of Britishpride with her offspring. (Photo: The Bulldog Club Inc.)

49

not bandy or curved. They should be rather short in proportion to the hind legs, but not so short as to make the back appear long, or detract from the dog's activity, and so cripple him. The elbows should be low and stand away from the ribs. The pasterns should be short and strong.

Body

The chest should be very wide, laterally round, prominent and deep, making the dog appear very broad and short-legged in front. The body should be well ribbed up behind, with the belly tucked up and not pendulous. The back should be short and strong, very broad at the shoulders, and comparatively narrow at the loins. There should be a slight fall to the back close behind the shoulders (its lowest part), whence the spine should rise to the loins (the top of which should be higher than the shoulders), thence curving again more suddenly to the tail, forming an arch – a distinctive characteristic of the breed – termed 'roach-back'.

Hindquarters

The legs should be large and muscular, and longer in proportion than the forelegs, so as to elevate the loins. The hocks should be slightly bent and well let down, so as to be long and muscular from the loins to the point of the hock. The lower part of the leg should be short, straight and strong. The stifles should be round and turned slightly outwards away from the body. The hocks are thereby made to approach each other, and the hind feet to turn outwards.

Feet

The hind feet, like the forefeet, should be round and compact, with the toes well split up and the knuckles prominent. The forefeet should be straight and turn very slightly outwards, of medium size and moderately round. The toes compact and thick, being well split up, making the knuckles prominent and high.

Tail

The tail, termed the 'stern', should be set on low, jut out rather than straight, then turn downwards. It should be round, smooth and devoid of fringe or coarse hair. It should be moderate in length – rather short than long – thick at the root and tapering quickly to a fine point. It

Skeleton of a Bulldog.

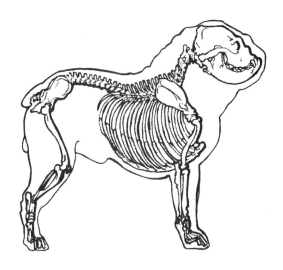

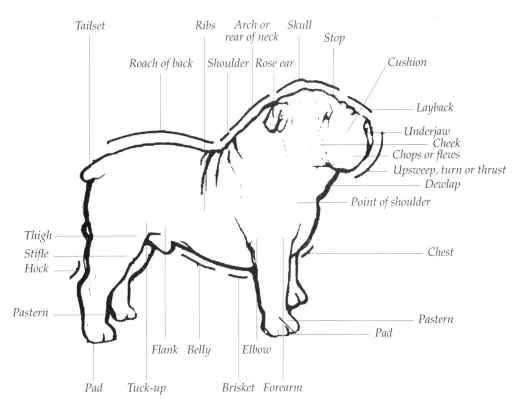

Points of the Bulldog.

should have a downward carriage (not having a decided upward curve at the end), and the dog should not be able to raise it over its back.

Coat

Should be fine in texture, short, close and smooth (hard only from the shortness and closeness, not wiry).

Colour

The colour should be whole or smut (that is, a whole colour with a black mask or muzzle). The only colours (which should be brilliant and pure of their sort) are whole colours, viz. – brindles, reds, with their varieties, fawns, fallows, etc., white and also pied (i.e. a combination of white with any other of the foregoing colours). Dudley, black, and black and tan are extremely undesirable colours.

Weight and Size

The most desirable weight for the Bulldog is 55 pounds for a dog and 50 pounds for a bitch.

The American Breed Standard

(Reproduced by kind permission of the American Kennel Club)

General Appearance, Attitude, Expression, etc.

The perfect Bulldog must be of medium size and smooth coat; with heavy, thick-set, low-swung body, massive short-faced head, wide shoulders and sturdy limbs. The general appearance and attitude should suggest great stability, vigor and strength. The disposition should be equable and kind, resolute and courageous (not vicious or aggressive), and demeanor should be pacific and dignified. These attributes should be countenanced by the expression and behavior.

Gait

The style and carriage are peculiar, his gait being a loose-jointed, shuffling, sidewise motion, giving the characteristic 'roll'. The action must, however, be unrestrained, free and vigorous

Proportion and Symmetry

The 'points' should be well distributed and bear good relation one to the other, no feature being in such prominence from either excess or lack of quality that the animal appears deformed or ill-proportioned.

Influence of Sex

In comparisons of different sex, due allowance should be made in favor of bitches, which do not bear the characteristics of the breed to the same degree of perfection and grandeur as do the dogs.

Size

The size for mature dogs is about 50 pounds; for mature bitches about 40 pounds.

Coat

The coat should be straight, short, flat, close, of fine texture, smooth and glossy. (No fringe, feather or curl.)

Color of Coat

The color of coat should be uniform, pure of its kind and brilliant. The various colors found in the breed are to be preferred in the following order: (1) red brindle, (2) all other brindles, (3) solid white, (4) solid red, fawn or fallow, (5) piebald, (6) inferior qualities of all the foregoing. **Note**: A perfect piebald is preferable to a muddy brindle or defective solid color. Solid black is very undesirable, but not so objectionable if occurring to a moderate degree in piebald patches. The brindles to be perfect should have a fine, even and equal distribution of the composite colors. In brindles and solid colors a small white patch on the chest is not considered detrimental. In piebalds the color patches should be well defined, of pure color and symmetrically distributed.

Skin

The skin should be soft and loose, especially at the head, neck and shoulders.

Wrinkles and Dewlap

The head and face should be covered with heavy wrinkles, and at the throat, from jaw to chest, there should be two loose pendulous folds, forming the dewlap.

Skull

The skull should be very large, and in circumference, in front of the ears, should measure at least the height of the dog at the shoulders. Viewed from the front, it should appear very high from the corner of the lower jaw to the apex of the skull, and also very broad and square. Viewed from the side, the head should appear very high, and very short from the point of the nose to the occiput. The forehead should be flat (not rounded or domed), neither too prominent nor overhanging the face.

Cheeks

The cheeks should be well rounded, protruding sideways and outward beyond the eyes.

Stop

The temples or frontal bones should be very well defined, broad, square and high, causing a hollow or groove between the eyes. This indentation, or stop should be both broad and deep and extend up the middle of the forehead, dividing the head vertically, being traceable to the top of the skull.

Eyes and Eyelids

The eyes, seen from the front, should be situated low down in the skull, as far from the ears as possible, and their corners should be in a straight line at right angles with the stop. They should be quite in front of the head, as wide apart as possible, provided their outer corners are within the outline of the cheeks when viewed from the front. They should be quite round in form, of moderate size, neither sunken nor bulging, and in color should be very dark. The lids should cover the white of the eyeball, when the dog is looking directly forward, and the lids should show no 'haw'.

Ears

The ears should be set high in the head, the front inner edge of each ear joining the outline of the skull at the top back corner of the skull, so as to place them as wide apart, and as high, and as far from the eyes as possible. The rose ear folds inward at its back lower edge, the upper front edge curving over, outward and backward, showing part of the inside of the burr. (The ears should not be carried erect or prick-eared or buttoned and should never be cropped.)

Face

The face, measured from the front of the cheekbone to the tip of the nose, should be extremely short, the muzzle being very short, broad, turned upward and very deep from the corner of the eye to the corner of the mouth.

Nose
The nose should be large, broad and black, its tip being set back deeply between the eyes. The distance from bottom of stop, between the eyes, to the tip of the nose should be as short as possible and not exceed the length from the tip of nose to the edge of underlip. The nostrils should be wide, large and black, with a well-defined line between them. Any nose other than black is objectionable and a brown or liver-colored nose shall disqualify.

Chops
The chops or 'flews' should be thick, broad, pendent and very deep, completely overhanging the lower jaw at each side. They join the under lip in front and almost or quite cover the teeth, which should be scarcely noticeable when the mouth is closed.

Jaws
The jaws should be massive, very broad, square and 'undershot', the lower jaw projecting considerably in front of the upper jaw and turning up.

Teeth
The teeth should be large and strong, with the canine teeth or tusks wide apart, and the six small teeth in front, between the canines, in an even, level row.

Neck

The neck should be short, very thick, deep and strong, and well arched at the back.

Shoulders

The shoulders should be muscular, very heavy, widespread and slanting outward, giving stability and great power.

Chest

The chest should be very broad, deep and full.

Brisket and Body

The brisket and body should be very capacious, with full sides, well-rounded ribs and very deep from the shoulders down to its lowest part, where it joins the chest. It should be well let down between the shoulders and the forelegs, giving the dog a broad, low, short-legged appearance. The body should be well ribbed up behind with the belly tucked up and not rotund.

Back

The back should be short and strong, very broad at the shoulders and comparatively narrow at the loins. There should be a slight fall in the back, close behind the shoulders (its lowest part), whence the spine should rise to the loins (the top of which should be higher than the top of the shoulders), thence curving again more suddenly to the tail, forming an arch (a very distinctive feature of the breed), termed 'roach back' or, more correctly, 'wheel back'.

Legs and Feet

Forelegs
The forelegs should be short, very stout, straight and muscular, set wide apart, with well-developed calves, presenting a bowed outline, but the bones of the legs should not be curved or bandy, nor the feet brought too close together.

Elbows
The elbows should be low and stand well out and loose from the body.

Hind Legs
The hind legs should be strong and muscular and longer than the forelegs, so as to elevate the loins above the shoulders. Hocks should

be slightly bent and well let down, so as to give length and strength from loins to hock. The lower leg should be short, straight and strong, with the stifles turned slightly outward and away from the body. The hocks are thereby made to approach each other, and the hind feet turn outward.

Feet
The feet should be moderate in size, compact and firmly set. Toes compact, well split up, with high knuckles and with short stubby nails. The front feet may be straight or slightly out-turned, but the hind feet should be pointed well outward.

Tail

The tail may either be straight or 'screwed' (but never curved or curly), and in any case must be short, hung low, with a decided downward carriage, thick root and fine tip. If straight, the tail should be cylindrical and of uniform taper. If 'screwed' the bends or kinks should be well defined, and they may be abrupt and even knotty, but no portion of the member should be elevated above the base or root.

Scale of Points

General Properties
Proportions and symmetry	5
Attitude	3
Expression	2
Gait	3
Size	3
Coat	2
Color of coat	4
	22

Head
Skull	5
Cheeks	2
Stop	4
Eyes and eyelids	3
Ears	5
Wrinkle	5
Nose	6

Chops	2
Jaws	5
Teeth	2
	39

Body, Legs, etc.

Neck	3
Dewlap	2
Shoulders	5
Chest	3
Ribs	3
Brisket	2
Belly	2
Back	5
Forelegs and elbows	4
Hind legs	3
Feet	3
Tail	4
	39

Grand Total	**100**

Disqualification

Brown or liver-colored nose

The UK Breed Standard

(Reproduced by kind permission of the Kennel Club)

General Appearance

Smooth-coated, thick set, rather low in stature, broad, powerful and compact. Head massive, fairly large in proportion to size, but no point so much in excess of others as to destroy the general symmetry, or make the dog appear deformed, or interfere with its powers of motion. Face short, muzzle broad, blunt and inclined upwards. Body short, well knit; limbs somewhat lighter in comparison with heavy foreparts. Bitches not so grand or well developed as dogs.

Top centre: this is the correct Bulldog outline. Good depth and width of foreface, a good barrel rib and plenty of brisket. Well off for bone. Nice 'tuck-up', well-angulated hindquarters with neat well let-down hocks. Note the strong neck, correct 'roach' topline with a good, neat tailset.

Middle left: this Bulldog has what is termed a 'Dippy' or 'Swampy' topline, usually accompanied by weak, straight hindquarters. This type of Bulldog usually appears 'Bum high'.

Middle right: this Bulldog is what is termed as 'Camel' backed. Not to be confused with the correct 'Roach'. The sharp drop at the withers makes the topline too pronounced, giving a 'hunched up' appearance.

Bottom left: this Bulldog is long in loin, the distance from the end of his ribcage to the rear legs. He is straight in topline and is long backed. When judging, most breed specialists allow a little for slightly longer backs in bitches. Many believe that they are better whelpers. Because of the length of back, some may be prone to hemivertibrae, a fusing of the small spinal bones.

Bottom right: this Bulldog is too short in back and is what we term as 'Stuffy'. This type of dog is usually straight in topline and hindquarters and has a high tailset. The short neck may lead to breathing difficulties in later life.

Ch. Bramor Tailor Maid, owned and bred by Brian and Mary Taylor.

Characteristics

Conveys impression of determination, strength and activity.

Temperament

Alert, bold, loyal, dependable, courageous, fierce in appearance, but possessed of an affectionate nature.

Head and Skull

Skull large in circumference, should measure round (in front of ears) approximately height of dog from shoulder. Viewed from the front appears very high from corner of lower jaw to apex of skull; also very broad and square. Cheeks well rounded and extending sideways beyond eyes. Viewed from the side, the head appears very high and short from back to point of nose. Forehead flat with skin upon and about head, loose, wrinkled, neither prominent nor overhanging face. Projections of frontal bones prominent, broad, square and high; deep wide indentation between eyes. From stop, a furrow, both broad and deep extending to the middle of the skull being traceable to apex. Face from front of cheekbone to nose, short, skin wrinkled. Muzzle short, broad, turned upwards and very deep from corner of eye to corner of mouth. Nose and nostrils large, broad and black, under no circumstances liver colour, red or brown; top set back towards eyes. Distance from the inner corner of eye (or from centre of stop between eyes) to extreme tip of nose not exceeding length from tip of nose to edge of underlip. Nostrils large and wide with well-defined vertical straight line between them. Flews (chops) thick, broad, pendent and very deep, hanging completely over the lower jaws at sides, not in front, joining underlip in front and quite covering teeth. Jaws broad, massive and square, lower jaw projecting considerably in front of upper and turning up. Viewed from front, the various properties of the face must be equally balanced on either side of an imaginary line down centre.

Eyes

Seen from front, situated low down in skull, well away from ears. Eyes and stop in same straight line, at right angles to furrow. Wide apart, but outer corners within the outline of cheeks. Round in shape, of moderate size, neither sunken nor prominent, in colour very dark – almost black – showing no white when looking directly forward.

Ears

Set high – i.e. front edge of each ear (as viewed from front) joins outline of skull at top corner of such outline, so as to place them as wide apart, as high and as far from eyes as possible. Small and thin. 'Rose ear' correct, i.e. folding inwards and back, upper or front inner edge curving outwards and backwards, showing part of inside of burr.

Mouth

Jaws broad and square with six small front teeth between canines in an even row. Canines wide apart. Teeth large and strong not seen when mouth closed. When viewed from front underjaw directly under upper jaw and parallel.

Neck

Moderate in length (rather short than long), very thick, deep and strong. Well arched back, with much loose, thick and wrinkled skin about throat, forming dewlap on each side, from lower jaw to chest.

Forequarters

Shoulders broad, sloping and deep, very powerful and muscular giving appearance of being 'tacked on' body. Brisket capacious, round and very deep from top of shoulders to lowest part where it joins chest. Well let down between forelegs. Large in diameter, round behind forelegs (not flat-sided, ribs well rounded). Forelegs very stout and strong, well developed, set wide apart, thick, muscular and straight, presenting a rather bowed outline, but bones of legs large and straight, not bandy nor curved and short in proportion to hind legs, but not so short as to make back appear long, or detract away from dog's activity and so cripple him. Elbows low and standing well away from ribs. Pasterns short, straight and strong.

Body

Chest wide, laterally round, prominent and deep. Back short, strong, broad at shoulders, comparatively narrower at loins. Slight fall to back close behind shoulders (lowest part) whence spine should rise to loins (top higher than top of shoulder), curving again more suddenly to tail, forming arch (termed roach back) – a distinctive characteristic of the breed. Body well-ribbed up behind with belly tucked up and not pendulous.

Hindquarters

Legs large and muscular, longer in proportion than forelegs, so as to elevate loins. Hocks slightly bent, well let down; leg long and muscular from loins to hock; short, straight, strong lower part. Stifles round and turned slightly outwards away from the body. Hocks thereby made to approach each other and hind feet to turn outwards.

Feet

Fore, straight and turning very slightly outward; of medium size and moderately round. Hind, round and compact. Toes compact and thick, well split up, making knuckles prominent and high.

Tail

Set on low, jutting out rather straight and then turning downwards. Round smooth and devoid of fringe or coarse hair. Moderate in length – rather short than long – thick at root, tapering quickly to a fine point. Downward carriage (not having a decided upward curve at the end) and never carried above the back.

Gait/Movement

Peculiarly heavy and constrained, appearing to walk with short, quick running steps on tips of toes, hind feet not lifted high, appearing to skim ground, running with one shoulder rather advanced.

Coat

Fine texture, short, close and smooth (hard only from shortness and closeness, not wiry).

Colour

Whole or smut (i.e. whole colour with black mask or muzzle, Only whole colours (which should be brilliant and pure of their sort) viz., brindles, reds with their various shades, fawns, fallows etc., white and pied (i.e. combination of white with any of the foregoing colours). Dudley, black, and black and tan highly undesirable.

Size

Dogs: 25kg (55lb); Bitches 22.7kg (50lb).

Faults

Any departure from the foregoing points should be considered a fault and the seriousness with which the fault should be regarded should be in exact proportion to its degree.

Note: Male animals should have two apparently normal testicles fully descended into the scrotum.

Interpretation of the Breed Standard

General Appearance and Characteristics

Of all domestic breeds of dog, the Bulldog is probably the most engineered by mankind. It would appear that in the early fighting dogs man found the desired temperament and then set about altering the body and shape to fit it. The body was kept short with the main weight in the ribcage up close to the head so that any sudden or violent shaking by the bull could not break the dog's back.

It is ironic that the Bulldog Club Inc. Standard of 1875 requires that, 'The dog should convey an impression of determination, strength and activity similar to that suggested by the appearance of a thickset Ayrshire bull' – the very animal he was originally designed to bait. The current Standard also asks for activity, but since they are very laid back, Bulldogs tend to be only as active as they want or need to be.

The Standard asks for a general appearance that is 'thick set, rather low in stature', which could be misunderstood to mean rather short in leg. In fact, when viewed front on, the distance between the legs

A Bulldog happily sharing his bed with a Pug and two Frenchies. Bulldogs are good mixers and, although compatible with other breeds, and dogs and cats, prefer the company of humans.

should appear to be equal to their length, so that the shape created by the dog's front is almost square. He should give the general impression of being a somewhat proud, dependable, almost condescending dog that has been built to last.

Temperament

The fierce appearance of the Bulldog belies his wonderfully affectionate nature. As the breed specialist Rowland Johns observed in his book *Our Friend The Bulldog* (Methuen & Co. Ltd, 1934), 'Not a noisy dog and not easily aroused, but when this happens he becomes a formidable and unyielding adversary.' Another specialist, Sidney H. Deacon, said in his book *Show Bulldogs* (Our Dogs Publishing Co. Ltd, 1906) 'he is slow to take offence and not easily aroused, and he never knows when he is beaten.'

Head, Skull and Points of the Face

The most important part of any Bulldog is the head. The old Standard allotted 45 out of 100 to the various head points. Overall balance is of great importance here as any obvious fault will throw all the other points out of kilter.

The conformation of the Bulldog's face, with the nose set back, enabled the dog to breathe whilst hanging on in the fray, and the creases and furrows allowed the blood to drain away from his eyes. The small, turned-back, 'rose-shaped' ears left little for the bull to get hold of, and the jaw, being undershot, acted like a torque wrench – the harder the bull's pull, the tighter the jaws' grip.

Oversized heads are termed 'bucket heads', and small ones 'pin heads'. There should be a reasonable amount of 'work' or wrinkle in the head: this should neither be gross, termed 'overdone'; nor lacking in wrinkle, termed 'plain in head'. When viewed straight on, the

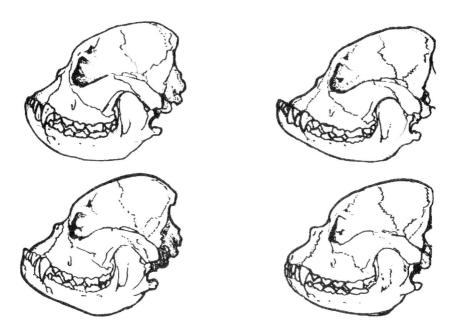

Detailed drawings of the Bulldog skull.
Top left: this is the correct skull with good fitting, slightly undershot jaw, allowing the dog to close its mouth without showing any teeth when viewed front on. Notice the good clean sweep and turn of the underjaw, known as the submaxillary bone.
Top right: this dog is very undershot with little thrust and turn of underjaw. He will probably also have a narrow spoon-shaped underjaw and will appear 'dish faced' from the side angle.
Bottom left: this dog has no turn or thrust of underjaw and his teeth will probably show when he is viewed front on with his mouth closed.
Bottom right: this dog has an even bite. Once again, no thrust or turn of underjaw, he will appear 'Pussy', 'Frog' or 'Monkey' faced.

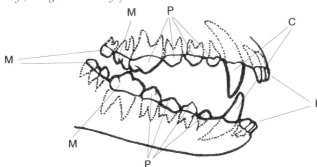

The Bulldog's jawbone showing the teeth. There should be six even incisors (I) between the canines (C) although they are seldom found in a straight line. The incisors tend to wear down quickly to small stumps in the adult Bulldog (M = molar; P = premolar).

foreface should be broad and well padded, and this should continue upwards, not converging in an imaginary 'A' shape. There should be a terrific sweep and turn of the underjaw and the whole head should convey the impression of everything turning and facing upwards.

The eyes should be dark, almost black, with no flecks or marbling. There should be no white or any haw showing when viewed head on; this is difficult as many Bulldogs lack some, if not all, pigment to the inner lids. The eye shape should be a good clean fit, neither loose nor dropping down (when it is termed a 'diamond eye').

The Standard asks for 'small and thin' ears, although very thin ears can have a tendency to be lively. The mouth should be a perfect fit, the lips meeting with no dentition showing.

Neck, Forequarters and Tail

When the Standard stipulates a moderate neck (rather short than long), it does not mean no neck at all: a Bulldog lacking in neck will often be more susceptible to breathing problems, so this is an important distinction to make.

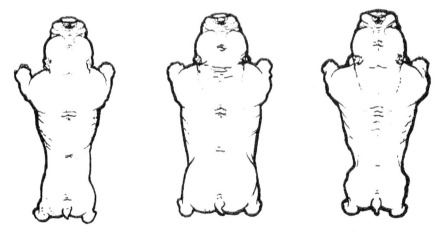

Left: this Bulldog is lacking in rib and when viewed overhead falls away behind the shoulders, allowing the judge to place his hand between the ribcage and the shoulderbone. The lack of rib will make the dog appear long in back.
Centre: this Bulldog is grossly overweight, making him appear 'stuffy'. He is also what is termed 'Beefy' or 'Bummy' behind, although one allows a little for this when judging the bitches.
Right: the correct outline showing good well tacked on shoulders, barrel of rib and the lovely 'Pear'-shaped body. The hindquarters are neat, strong and well muscled.

Left: these hindquarters are weak, finely boned and inverted, termed as 'Cow Hocked'.
Centre: here is the reverse, once again finely boned, termed as 'Barrel Hocked'.
Right: the correct back end. Strong, well boned with neat, well let down hocks. Remember, the Bulldog skims, not drives, from behind.

Left: this is the correct front. This Bulldog is 'square', well boned and will move his width in front on the move. Note the good depth of chest and that the shoulders are 'tacked on', not underneath, his ribcage.
Centre: this Bulldog looks quite typical and is well off for bone. However, he is a little upright in shoulder and the legs are underneath his ribcage, something termed as 'tight in front'. On the move he will 'pin in', giving an untypical gait.
Right: this Bulldog is what is termed as 'out at elbow', commonly known as the 'Queen Anne front'. This type of front is normally accompanied with loose, splayed feet. On the move, he will throw his pasterns causing him to move in an untypical fashion, known as 'Crabbing'.

The bones of the leg should be straight and the foot slightly turned out, not bowed. A bowed leg, termed 'Queen Anne', is incorrect. The width between the legs and the height of the leg should form a square, with the brisket dropping down into it.

Gay or lively tails spoil the overall outline of the dog. The tail should never be carried proud of the topline.

Movement

A Bulldog should walk towards you on the tips of his toes and on a slight angle, leading with one shoulder. He should move his width in front and not flick his pasterns, either inwards or outwards: the 1875 Standard's comparison with a horse cantering is a descriptive one. His hind action should be light and skimming. Unlike many breeds, Bulldogs do not drive from behind. However, he should not move too closely behind (when the hocks almost meet or stab the ground in a stilted manner).

Comparing the Standards

When studying the required conformation of the Bulldog, it is well worth looking at all three of the standards reproduced here: comparison helps to clarify the various points. However, it is also interesting to note the differences.

The UK Standard stipulates that the Bulldog's movement should be 'peculiarly heavy and constrained'. While the American Standard agrees that it should be peculiar, it also states clearly that should be 'unrestrained, free and vigorous' – a complete contrast. The colour black is considered highly undesirable in the UK Standard, whereas the American Standard will accept it if it occurs to a moderate degree in piebald patches.

The most obvious difference, though, is in the weight: the UK Standard specifies a weight of 25kg (55lb) for a dog and 22.7kg (50lb) for a bitch (as did the 1875 Standard); the US Standard specifies a lesser weight of 50lb for a dog and 40lb for a bitch. And when you take into account that most winning stock in the UK today would probably exceed the UK Standard's figure by at least 5lb, the difference is even more marked.

3

Selecting Your Dog

Why a Bulldog?

One of Britain's leading weekly canine newspapers once invited me to participate in a Bulldog Forum at which I would answer questions from an audience. At one point I was asked, 'What do you particularly like about the breed's character and temperament?' Where do you start with this humorous, affectionate aristocrat of the dog world? Always guaranteed to provoke a response, no other breed comes even close, and every Bulldog owner could fill a book with his praises. Fashion guru and 'Emperor of Excess', the late Gianni Versace was once quoted as saying that his clothes were for people with big egos. Bulldogs, being such exaggerated characterful dogs, are similarly not for the faint hearted. So be prepared for attention wherever and whenever you go.

Even their vulnerability endears you to them. This is one of, if not the most, resilient of breeds, under threat since its inception, coming from the most disreputable and dubious past as a common fighting dog to be the companion of the fashionable and the elite.

Many of society's artists, celebrities, and top sports people have been drawn to this mesmeric breed, among them (to name only a few), Andre Agassi, Truman Capote, Captain and Tennille, HSH Princess Caroline of Monaco, George Clooney, Divine, George Forman, Nigel Kennedy, Jayne

Football star Kevin Keegan with Ch. Jacob of Kelloe at the Abbey Road Studios, 1986.

Celebrity fundraising in Battersea Park with Joan Greenwood, Julia McKenzie and David Kernan, 1984. (Photo: 'Pro-Dogs'.)

Mansfield, Olivia Newton John, Peter O'Toole and Sian Phillips, Pablo Picasso and his daughter Paloma, Lee Sharpe, Brooke Shields, Sylvester Stallone, Roger Whittaker, Hank Williams and Tennessee Williams. The long list continues with the Governor of Hawaii Ben Gayatano, US Senator and former presidential contender Barry Goldwater, and the late Earl Mountbatten of Burma, who had many family photographs taken with his Bulldog on the lawns of Government House during his final years as Viceroy of India. Major Melling (former Curator of the Crown Jewels) bought one of our Jacob's sired puppies in the late 1980s, and the young dog became a well-known figure among the Beefeaters at the Tower of London. As the Tower's ravens have their wings clipped, and yet mate on the wing, they are renowned for being bad-tempered and frustrated during the mating season, so we had to keep the young puppy until he was too heavy for the birds to carry him up and away.

Having said all this, it is important to acknowledge that the Bulldog is not necessarily the right choice for everyone, and any prospective owner should think long and heard before deciding on the breed. Make sure that he fits the picture of the dog you are looking for. If you want a dog for lengthy, brisk walks, or a live wire, constantly at your beck and call, a Bulldog is not for you. For while he can keep up with the best he just cannot or will not sustain it. Bulldogs are companion dogs, and in this respect they compensate admirably for any apparent lack of performance. They need love and human companionship to prosper, kindness tempered with firmness. Generally I have found them to be very intelligent dogs although, as with all breeds, intelligence will differ greatly from one individual to the next, and I consider a dog's environment to be an important contributory factor in the development of his intelligence. Bulldogs are not generally barkers. They are usually very quiet; although they do snore, which I find relaxing and reassuring. They sometimes belch and occasionally suffer from flatulence. When they yawn, their heads quite often appear to be hinged in the middle, and when they lie

Bulldogs make excellent companions for children. (Photo: Simon Lathan.)

upside down they look like hammerhead sharks.

One of the Bulldog's most obvious attributes must be his adaptability. He is perfectly suited to twentieth-century living. He will quite happily live in a high-rise block or a twenty-acre farm. Little and often is the case when it comes to exercise but many, such as my own tribe, walk for miles each day on the Sussex Downs. Bulldogs love travelling in cars and quite often at the journey's end I have to shake them to wake them. Because of their short-backed conformation they cannot curl up like most other breeds, so they sleep either in a flat, prone position, with their paws and feet out, or on their sides. Often you will notice that while sleeping they will gently push their front paws back and forth. This is a habit left over from the time when they suckled from their mother, massaging the teats to make the milk flow.

If you already have pets there should be no problem introducing a Bulldog into the family. He will be inquisitive and friendly. Bulldogs usually mix well with other pets, including cats, especially if they are introduced while still a puppy.

If you know of anyone who has owned a Bulldog or knows of a breeder, past or present, contact that person and talk about the various aspects of the breed. Not only will you have a better idea of whether the breed will suit you, but you may get some good advice on where to find the right puppy.

Puppy or Adult

Once the decision to own a Bulldog has been made, most families choose to buy a puppy as it means that both dog and children can spend their formative years together. Many people, especially in their later years, prefer the idea of a slightly more mature Bulldog. They may feel that they have neither the time nor the inclination to go through the rigmarole of house-training, and the very elderly may feel that buying a puppy would be unfair as the dog may have twelve years or more of healthy active life ahead.

Opportunities to buy a mature dog do sometimes present themselves. Breeders will occasionally part with an adult, and Bulldogs are fortunate in having a well-organized, efficient rescue service. However, many of the Bulldogs here may have had past behavioural or health problems, or maybe a history of ill-treatment or neglect. Such dogs require very careful consideration in being placed, and for this reason I feel that rescue dogs are better placed with, if not Bulldog lovers, then dog people, who will have some experience and know-how.

Male or Female

The Bulldog is one of the few breeds in which often the males are more affectionate than the bitches. Many people choose a bitch because they fancy the idea of breeding a litter of their own at some later date, but unless you are quite certain of this, and prepared to give up a lot of sleepless nights, consider carefully. The breed is well known for complications in whelping and rearing – a minefield for the uninitiated breeder – and in addition there is the responsibility of placing the pups in loving, caring homes.

Remember, a Bulldog bitch will have two very heavy seasons each year, giving off a strong odour. She may have to be confined. Bitches can also be quite sparky, especially with other bitches. I have known bitches, often mother and daughter, share a kennel or home in perfect harmony for a number of years only to fall out badly over something trivial, such as a windfall apple or favourite toy and have to be separated permanently.

If you decide on a male puppy you will need to ensure that he has two testicles fully descended into the scrotum; such a dog is termed 'entire'. Some males will have both testicles descended at six weeks, although for most it will occur between eight and ten weeks. If either one or both testicles are not down by, say, sixteen weeks it is advisable to contact your vet. A dog that is not entire will not be able to take part in shows and will be an unlikely prospect for breeding at a later date. It is unusual for the dog not to have testicles at all; it is usually that they have been unable to pass through the ring into the scrotum. In later life these can strangulate and eventually become cancerous. For this reason, a vet will usually prefer to remove them when the dog reaches maturity.

The choice between dog and bitch is ultimately a personal one, but it is worth remembering that a dog will remain sexually active throughout his entire life, whereas a bitch, unless she is in season, will be more or less sexless.

Buying a Dog for Stud

Those new to the breed or dog breeding in general are often under the misapprehension that if they buy a male they can use him for stud work. Unless a dog is 'born in the purple', that is he is a litter-brother to a top champion who in turn is tightly linebred, or he has displayed himself with flying colours in the show ring he is unlikely to conjure up much interest from good breeders. Even then, most stud dogs will not produce progeny that is successful in the show ring.

Finding a Puppy

First and foremost, try to purchase your puppy from a reputable breed-er with a history of producing good, healthy stock. Remember there is no such thing as Victorian Bulldogs, Jubilee Bulldogs, Sussex Bulldogs, English or British Bulldogs. I have read articles on Olde English Bull-dogs, Bordeaux Bulldogs, American Bulldogs, Old Country Bulldogs, Old English White, and Alapaha Blue Blood Bulldogs! Members of the breed are known simply as Bulldog, nothing more, nothing less. If they are advertised under exotic names, they are probably just mongrels or, at best, crossbreeds. Take care as it is commonly believed that the first thing to suffer when crossing Bulldogs is the temperament.

Many years ago a renowned dog person, Clifford Derwent, pro-duced Bulldog crosses that he named Regency Bulldogs. He believed that his breeding programme would lead to fitter, healthier specimens. However, the temperament suffered so much that many of them had to be fed at the end of a pole. Clifford wisely abandoned the exercise.

Before starting out on your search, it is well worth doing some homework. Study, read and absorb any-thing on Bulldogs that you can lay your hands on; talk with all and sundry; and be prepared to embark on a life-time's learning experience.

A champion and a future champion: Ch. Kelloe Angel Dust with his son, Ch. Medbull Gold Dust Over Kelloe.

73

The Kennel Club

The Kennel Club is helpful here and can sometimes supply, if not a comprehensive list of breeders, recent detailed information of local Bulldog clubs and show secretaries. These in turn will send information of any local matches, puppy competitions or Limit, Open or Championship shows. Here you can ask around, and make yourself known to breeders and exhibitors, many of whom may know of recent litters.

The Press

Next stop is the weekly dog press, in the UK *Dog World* and *Our Dogs* (the oldest weekly canine newspaper in the world). These will carry breeders' advertisements, normally towards the back, and in any event will have specialist Bulldog breed-note writers. They will know of all the most recent events – births, deaths and up-to-date show results – and most give a contact telephone number at the foot of their columns. As well as the weeklies there are numerous monthly glossy publications, most with breeders' listings.

Pet Shops

Most reputable pet shops have stopped selling pedigree dogs over the counter. In any case, this was never the right way to buy a puppy. Many

now act as agencies instead, dealing with bona fide breeders whom they have known over many years and can put you in touch with. Always try to visit the home or kennel of the breeder and ask to see the mother (dam) along with the other sibling brothers and sisters. Naturally the mother will not be looking her best having reared a litter, and it may not be possible to see the father at all as many breeders

Two pups from the same litter. (Photo: Simon Lathan.)

travel huge distances in order to use the best stud-dog. Having said this, be suspicious if you are at all times refused access to view the dam; most reputable breeders will be happy for you to visit by appointment.

Puppy Farms

A puppy farm is a breeding establishment whose sole purpose is to make high profits. This means that the standard of ante-natal and post-natal care must necessarily be quite poor, for the proper management of a brood-bitch and her puppies is labour-intensive and frequently expensive. Furthermore, in order to earn her keep, a bitch will be bred from far more often than is healthy either for her or her future off-spring. One of the main things to suffer is the all-important process of socializing the puppies with human beings. Research has shown that puppies that come from puppy farms after fourteen weeks of age found it very difficult to settle as a household pet. They had received so little human contact that they had established bad behavioural patterns and could only really ever relate to other dogs.

Puppy farms normally advertise in the large, national weekly newspapers that sell everything from houses to livestock and cars. They may also use unscrupulous pet shop dealers to contact potential buyers. In an effort to exert some control over this kind of breeder – while at the same time trying to avoid hindering genuine breeders – the Kennel Club has introduced strict regulations that limit the frequency and the number of litters that can legitimately be registered out of any one bitch, and that restricts the age at which a bitch may be allowed to breed.

For this reason it is extremely important to check the documentation very carefully. How bona fide is the pedigree? This kind of breeder will make concerted efforts to get round Kennel Club rules, so you must be alert. It goes without saying that you should never buy a puppy with no documents at all.

What to Look For

Buying a Puppy for Show

Initially, most people say that they only want a pet! However, this can often be short-sighted, as quite often they will be bitten by the show bug and need to find an additional Bulldog puppy. Potential buyers often feel that the prices will become inflated if they enquire about

From eight-week-old puppy ...

show stock. But be honest with the breeder. Many potential show dogs have languished in pet homes, while on the other hand it is unfair to an established breeder when a dog they sold in good faith, solely as a companion, makes its way into the show ring.

Whatever your ultimate aim or ambitions, you basically want a puppy that conforms as much as possible to the Breed Standard, something typical that actually looks like a Bulldog. After all, that is why you have chosen the breed.

More often than not, all the preconceived ideas about the type of puppy the family are looking for go right out of the window the moment they are confronted with an entire litter. That outgoing pup that melts all hearts may turn out to be hyperactive, while the bashful, quiet little soul that shuns affection and stands his ground in the corner, may prove to be a shy, introverted and nervous adult.

I have always maintained that the age of six to eight weeks is the best time to judge a puppy. If the pups are less than stunning at this most attractive age, be wary. Many breeders believe that a puppy at this age is

a miniature of how he will eventually finish as an adult. Remember that a puppy that is long in back, or has a nose, or lacks rib and general substance, is unlikely to improve with age. Check the texture and condition of the coat. Bear in mind that a skilful

... to winning show bitch: St. Levan's Minnie the Moocher. (Photos: Simon Lathan.)

Eight-week-old puppies. (Photo: Simon Lathan.)

handler can make a mediocre puppy appear to be a different dog, stretching it into all possible show stances and telling you this is correct. Let the puppy wander around on his own accord, watch him stand naturally, and make your own judgement. Lastly, remember that at the end of the day there is no such thing as a show puppy, just a promising puppy with show potential.

Body Shape

In my opinion, body shape is indicative of personality. High on leg, narrow-through, rangy types are more often than not extremely active, whereas the heavy-boned, stocky, plodding puppy will have a corresponding character – generally quieter and laid back. Whatever the slight differences between the shape of one puppy and another, look for a well-boned, stocky, plodding puppy that is fairly outgoing and active. If possible, enlist the help of an experienced breeder who will notice faults, including the minor ones that will preclude the puppy from any sort of show career at some later date. Many lines tend to differ greatly in the speed at which they reach maturity, so look for a less exaggerated, overdone puppy. Here you will have to rely on the advice of the breeder, as he will be the only person who really knows how quickly his line matures.

Head

Ensure that the eyes are clear, bright and dark, with no inner lids or white of the eye showing when viewed straight on. If there is a fleck, or any kind of marbling, this will only become more pronounced as the dog matures. Light or blue eyes are unacceptable in the Breed Standard and, although this will not affect the dog's general health, you will not be able to show him or expect to breed from this kind of stock.

The nose should be black and the nostrils wide and large. Pink or brown patches on the nose (a 'butterfly nose') usually fill in eventually, but this can take up to a year and looks rather unattractive.

The Standard calls for rose ears, that is ears held back showing the burr. However, most Bulldog pups' ears will still hang forward at eight to nine weeks, and these are termed 'buttoned ears'. The ears' muscles are extremely delicate and one should avoid playing with them; as the muscles strengthen, the ear should turn back of its own accord. If you experience any problems, it is advisable to contact an experienced breeder who will use a latex -based adhesive to secure the ears temporarily in the correct position. The adhesive quickly wears off and is quite harmless. Sometimes this practice raises eyebrows, but it really does work.

Tails

Bulldog tails are never docked, so avoid extremely tight screw tails, as these can lead to problems such as wet eczema in later life. Straight or long tails are not always the answer as these have been known to sit too tightly at the base against the rectum, resulting in similar problems. Tail carriage is another factor. High-set or high-held tails (termed 'gay'), spoil the balance and outline of the topline. There again, a high proportion of high-held tails balance themselves out in later months as the puppy matures. The correct tail should never be carried proud of the topline.

Colour

Generally speaking, from the show angle, colour is cosmetic and unimportant. It is a breed where breeding to colour can be difficult. The most popular colours are red and white, brindle and white, white, white-ticked, white pied, and fawn or smut. These last two colours are the most likely to duplicate if bred to each other. Solid colours can appear strange and rather unattractive, while brindles can create the optical illusion that the dog lacks straight bone. More often than not, complete litters will be like a chocolate box with all puppies having totally different colours and markings. Remember your final choice should be an overall balance and conformation; a good colour is a bonus.

Collecting your Puppy

Once you have decided on a particular puppy and the sale is agreed, arrange to collect him some time during the day when it is light. Collecting during darkness is even more stressful for the puppy, as this

A five-week-old litter basking in the fresh air.

will not only be the first time he has been apart from his litter-brothers and sisters but probably the only time he has been outside the house where he was born. Make sure that you are accompanied so that the puppy can perhaps sit on a lap or be nursed during the journey, and take plenty of paper towels and moist wipes.

Along with the official documentation, the breeder should provide you with a diet sheet listing not only his usual food but also any important additives such as vitamins and bonemeal that he may need to continue with. Ask the breeder for advice on the brands of food and types of water bowl they recommend. It is always an excellent idea to obtain from the breeder a couple of bags of the puppy's regular food, or at least enough for the first few days. In addition, take a container and fill it with local tap water, since water hardness and softness varies greatly from area to area. This is something that for the most part is generally overlooked but must account for many cases of looseness and diarrhoea in young puppies.

The same litter at ten weeks returning from the vet's after their second vaccinations.

Ask the breeder when the puppy was last wormed, and also which particular product was used. This information can then be passed on to your own vet, who will advise on which wormer should be used. Worm larvae are present in the pups from birth, so this is important, although it is easily controlled by simple treatments that are available in powder, tablet, or even paste form.

When you pay for the puppy, agree with the breeder that you will have your vet give the pup the once-over some time within the next forty-eight hours. Enquire as to whether the puppy has suffered any illness and what treatment he received. Your vet will check the dog's general health and look for problems undetected by you or the breeder, such as heart murmurs and respiratory problems.

Papers

You will need to make sure that you receive all the relevant documents. This is important not just to ensure that there will be no difficulty with pursuing future showing or breeding plans, but to reassure yourself: no reputable breeder will sell you a dog with no papers. These should include:

1. **A receipt.**
2. **Your puppy's pedigree**. This shows the names of the puppy's sire and dam and, usually those of three generations before them. Always check that details such as sex, colour and date of birth are correct.
3. **Registration form.** The registration must be with the Kennel Club and no other body. Check that the registration form has been signed on the reverse and that there are no endorsements – that is, restrictions imposed by the breeder when the puppy was initially registered, such as a block on breeding, or export, or changing the puppy's name. If these apply then the breeder is duty bound to tell you when purchasing the Bulldog, and it is probable that the breeder will ask you to confirm in writing that you were aware of any restrictions at the time of purchase.
4. **Vaccination certificate**. If the puppy has not yet received his first vaccination, you should be aware of this so that you can have it done at the correct time.
5. If the puppy has received any veterinary treatment (other than vaccinations), this should ideally be specified in writing, as the information may be required either by your own vet or by any company with whom you might decide to take out insurance on your puppy.

4

Puppy Care and Management

Confine your new puppy to a certain area of the house, somewhere where there is some life, human contact, people cooking, washing, and so on. The kitchen is ideal as it is usually quite warm and there is normally direct access to the garden or patio. Place him in a secure draught-free area from which he can explore and familiarize himself with his new environment. Do not leave him alone while you spend long periods elsewhere in the house. Talk to him and reassure him, and he will settle quite quickly.

House Rules

The first night away from his siblings can be traumatic for you as well as the puppy. Hot-water bottles, wrapped in towelling are useful as they will ripple, resembling the puppy's mother's movement; and a clock or radio emitting low-key sounds will help to settle and reassure him. Make sure the hot-water bottle is securely wrapped.

At some stage during the night, he will more often than not cry out and it is difficult to resist the temptation to gather him up and place him in or next to your bed. This is a mistake: it will set a precedent that will cease to be so appealing when he is fully grown.

No Climbing or Jumping

Bulldogs' shoulders are tacked on, that is placed on to the sides of the chest and not underneath it. This means that the muscles are quite fragile and tender during their formative, growing months, and in no circumstances should you allow your puppy either to climb or to jump. For this reason we never allow our Bulldogs to climb on furniture or attempt to scale the stairs. Climbing stairs is the easy bit: getting back down is another matter. If, for whatever reason, your puppy has managed to get up, pick him up and carry him back down to base.

Never allow him to descend under his own steam. If your puppy damages his shoulder it could take weeks, sometimes months, to repair.

Equipment and Accessories

Bedding

The oval, plastic dog beds seem the most practical as they are relatively chew-resistant, draught-proof, and easily cleaned when the puppy has an accident. Because of the Bulldog's short-backed conformation, he cannot curl up as other breeds do, so it is important to make sure that the bed you choose provides sufficient room for your puppy to lie either on his side or outstretched. Oval or rectangular beds are ideal, but unfortunately Bulldog puppies soon outgrow the smaller sizes and will be swamped in an adult bed. Line the bed with something comfortable to sleep on. The imitation sheepskin or 'Vetbed' is the most practical bedding to use as it is chew-resistant, and can be washed and dried quickly. It is non-absorbent, so it has the added advantage that it will dry if the puppy has an accident.

Foldable Cages

Years ago when I first started showing, dogs were placed on bedding on the show benches and their collars attached to a ring by what was called a benching chain. This was quite unsatisfactory as many a time a Bulldog would lunge at a passing dog purely out of curiosity and half-strangle himself, from dangling off the side of the bench. Wire folding cages made their appearance during the early 1980s and are now an indispensable part of dog showing.

The correct measurements for an adult dog are 24in (61cm) high, 22in (56cm) wide, and 28in (71cm) long. This size fits perfectly into the standard-size show bench provided for Bulldogs by show societies. It will also fit perfectly into the back of an estate or hatchback car, and will stop the dog from being thrown around in the back space when the car is braking or cornering. If you stop for fuel or whatever, it is reassuring to know that the temptation to chew the car's interior cannot be indulged. Also, at shows, you have the added bonus of being able to lock the cage and know your dog is secure.

The Bulldog likes the security of a cage. It makes a good overnight kennel for the new puppy, and a good place in which to confine him when he feels the need to empty his bladder or bowels, or has a sudden urge to sink his razor-sharp teeth into the kitchen units.

Toys and Chews

Toys are important if your puppy is going to be on his own, perhaps for the first time, for any period of time. They will not only serve to occupy him but they will help with his teething.

I always prefer the hard nylon or rubber washable types of dog toy, available from your local pet shop or at dog shows. Make sure that these are too large for the puppy to swallow, although you will still need to watch that he does not break off small pieces that could inadvertently be ingested.

Avoid the hard, leathery, hide chews as these will quickly become slimy and, if swallowed, could easily choke the dog. Hard sterilized marrow bones are safe, but I never, ever allow my dogs natural bones to chew once their second set of teeth are through at the age of about five months. Some maintain that constant chewing of hard bones is often the cause of wry mouths. My view is that this is a congenital problem, but I have experienced a young adult breaking his canines while chewing hard objects.

To my thinking, a broken canine is really the finish of a Bulldog's show career. My breed-record winning bitch Ch. Kelloe White Glove's beautiful little sister broke one of her canines clean off whilst a junior, and I never showed her after that (although she fortunately excelled herself as a brood-bitch, producing for me Ch. Kelloe Truly Madly Deeply and Eng. & Ital. Ch. Kelloe Angel Dust). Having said that, showing a dog with broken canines is largely a matter of choice. Some judges may wish to overlook it as just another fault, and I have known several breeders campaign dogs with broken, or in one case, two broken canines to their championship titles (one of the dogs winning Challenge Certificates into double figures).

The most dangerous 'chews' are chicken bones, or any bones that have been cooked. Some would argue that in their natural habitat, dogs would gnaw at the bones of their prey, but these are at least raw. Most bones available from pet shops are of the cooked variety, which are brittle and easily splintered, and extremely dangerous if swallowed.

Feeding Utensils
Food and water bowls should be large enough for your puppy to feed comfortably, but not so large that the puppy risks falling into them.

Hygiene is important, so they should be easy to clean. Bear in mind that, light, flimsy bowls are easily knocked over.

Collar and Lead

The newcomer to Bulldogs will often feel a temptation to splash out on an extremely smart collar and ID tag. Bulldogs are never that keen on having anything around their necks, probably because they are generally broader and shorter in this region than most other breeds. I have found that they excel at doing a 'Houdini', and the most securely fitted collars have often been found the next morning, chewed beyond recognition. Two Bulldogs together will often work in unison to achieve the same end, so as a rule I wouldn't bother.

The occasions when your puppy has to wear a collar and lead, I would recommend the nylon show-type lead that slips easily over the head and on to the neck, and is tightened with a metal clip. These are sold in reputable pet shops. (In any case, conventional collars are unsuitable for puppies because of the rapid rate of growth: you would have to replace them on an almost weekly basis.)

One restraint that I particularly dislike is the harness favoured by the Staffordshire Bull Terrier people. They look great on Staffies but are unsuitable for the Bulldog's large chest and brisket. My stud-dog Tugga Tough Decision for Kelloe used to prefer a scarf tied around his neck, and when he knew we were going for a stroll he would wait patiently while I chose that day's particular colour. He became a familiar sight in Chelsea Kings Road as he paraded up and down, the original Boulevardier!

Inoculations

The new puppy's inoculations are given in two parts. Most vets prefer to give the first injection at either eight or ten weeks, and the second two weeks later. It is then considered prudent to wait a further two weeks before allowing your puppy to venture into the outside world.

The standard inoculations protect your puppy from distemper, hepatitis, leptospirosis, and parvovirus (*see* Infectious Diseases in Chapter 10), but in order for the protection to continue, you must return the dog each year for a reinforcing booster. On initial inoculation you will be issued with a vaccination certificate, which will be updated at every booster. Veterinary practices usually send out reminders when the time for a booster is near.

Feeding

Good food and diet can assist in helping the development of a potentially good puppy, but it will make little difference to a poor-quality one. By the time that you collect your puppy, he should be on five meals a day. At about twelve weeks, this is reduced to four meals, and by the time he is six months old, he will be on two a day. Many owners feed their dogs just once a day. I think this is rather unkind; after all, would you want to eat just one meal a day? My dogs are fed twice daily and given biscuits before they retire each night.

Always ensure that there are copious amounts of accessible fresh water at all times, and empty and replenish the bowls each morning. Rats and other animals frequently drink from water bowls at night and, since rats' urine carries leptospirosis, it is very important to scrub any outdoor bowls first thing every morning regardless of whether you think the water may have been contaminated.

You may find that your puppy is less inclined to be greedy with food now that he is eating alone and not in competition with his siblings, but if he seems completely off his food you should have him checked by the vet. Give your puppy as much food as he wants. I like to see a roly-poly puppy with a good layer of fat on him. You can always take weight off; getting it back is another matter. As with humans, some live to eat, others eat to live.

Grooming

It is a good idea to get your puppy accustomed to the grooming brush and nail clippers at an early age. This will help to prevent problems later when longer grooming sessions will be undertaken (*see* Chapter 5). You will in any case need to check the puppy's nails every week. At this age, the nails grow very quickly and, in the weeks before and just after the puppy's inoculations, he will not be walking on street pavements and wearing them down naturally. Keep an especially close eye on the dew-claws which, owing to their position on the lower leg, receive no natural wear at all. Clip off just the tips of the nails using a pair of nail clippers. Most crucially of all, you must clean your puppy's face every day. This is not something that you can afford to do only occasionally, and you must encourage your puppy to accept it. More detailed guidance to nail clipping and face cleaning is given in Chapter 5.

It is also a good idea to get into the habit of checking your puppy's ears and mouth. A puppy who is used to being examined in this way will be more accepting of a vet's or future show judge's inspection. And, of course, if you find anything amiss, it can be dealt with before it becomes a major problem.

Basic Training

I once overheard a fellow dog breeder say that the first rule in successful dog training is to be smarter than the dog. Which is why, he explained, some breeds are easier to train than others.

There are two distinctly different types of formal training: obedience and ringcraft (*see* Chapter 6). By virtue of its very nature, obedience does not immediately appeal to a level-headed Bulldog. He will usually be less than enthusiastic in doing anything unless he is either in the mood or can see a valid reason for it. Although I have known many, albeit patient, owners who have taken up obedience with marked success.

Having said all this, everyone appreciates a well-behaved, responsive dog. A companion Bulldog should be taught to walk happily on the lead, to be clean in the house, to be under control, and not to chase or be assertive or aggressive towards other dogs, cats, and animals in general.

Training lessons should be carried out on a daily basis, and each one should be short so that they do not become tedious. Try to make them

Print 1822: 'How to train a Bull Dog.'

an enjoyable experience, away from the traffic and other distractions. When keeping (or 'running on' as it is termed) two or more puppies from the same litter or of similar age, it is most important to split them up for walking or training purposes. Otherwise they will distract each other, and you will experience great difficulty at some later stage when they have to walk and be handled on their own.

Remember that every puppy is an individual, so be prepared to adapt your approach to suit. The formula that is successful in one case may not necessarily work in another. You may have had a previous dog whose outgoing, exuberant nature took all your energy to control and calm down, but this new arrival may differ totally, requiring a softer, more laid-back approach.

In educating the Bulldog, the trainer should be seeking obedience, while at the same time encouraging the dog's unique personality to shine through. When showing, it might be considered a great advantage to have an exhibit that stands like a statue as the judge goes over him. But then the picture falls apart when the dog is required to move and goes from the end of the ring to the other plodding in a lifeless manner, totally lacking animation. Some of the breed's greatest dogs are more often remembered for their outgoing extrovert personalities, enhanced a by an attentive, skilled handler. So it is important that you do not pursue absolute, perfect obedience at the expense of the dog's character. Natural dog handlers are the exception rather than the rule. The main thing is to be consistent, for your Bulldog will acquire bad habits every bit as fast as good ones.

Your Bulldog will never understand what you are saying but he will learn to recognize the volume and the tone of your voice. A firm 'No' will soon be understood as you both come to accept what you expect of each other. Never allow your Bulldog to jump up at people: check this habit from an early age. It may not bother you but those standing in ruined or stained clothes and, perhaps, laddered tights may feel otherwise.

House-Training

When you collect your puppy at around eight weeks of age, the breeder will probably have started some form of newspaper training. So place newspaper next to the door to the garden and encourage your puppy to use it. As soon as he has eaten, a young puppy will want to urinate or defecate or both, (something we term 'clean himself'). You will notice a marked change in his behaviour as he anxiously moves back and forth at a faster than normal speed, almost as if he is looking for something. Immediately you see this happening, place him on to the paper, and watch over him so that as soon as he has finished you can lavish him with praise – something he will soon learn to look forward to. If the weather is fine place him straight outside rather than on the paper, and follow the same procedure, always remembering to make a fuss of him when he goes in the right place.

When an accident occurs refrain from smacking him. This is a pointless exercise. He will soon get used to the volume and the tone of your voice, and these are ultimately a far more effective deterrent; after all, if he misbehaves on the other side of the room, none of us have arms six feet long! At night, especially for the first few weeks, it might be an idea to place him and his bedding in a small pen, lined with newspaper, as in the darkness he may experience some difficulty in finding the door.

The length of time it will take to house-train your puppy fully will largely depend on the amount of time, effort and energy that you are prepared to put into it. You can gradually introduce him to other areas of the house, between feeding times, when there is less chance of an accident. By twelve weeks you will gradually begin to decrease the amount of meals and, by six months, he should be down to two meals a day, and this will undoubtedly help. Perseverance is of the utmost importance. I have known some owners house-train their puppies within days, and lackadaisical ones take months!

Lead Training

This is something that can be traumatic when you first start, and because of this there is a general tendency to put it off. We normally start at around seven to eight weeks. Begin by loosely putting a nylon show lead over the puppy's head, and then let him play around for a while. He will gradually get used to the idea, but the name of the game is to make it fun, and not to spend too long on it on any occasion.

Always conduct these sessions in familiar surroundings, in the home or the garden or yard, and he will soon become comfortable trotting around on his lead. It is important that he feels safe and secure, there is no point in taking him out and about in a strange environment where there might be buses and trains, or any number of other frightening objects. Just getting used to the lead is quite enough to deal with at this stage.

Keep a close eye on him and be patient and reassuring. Later in life the young Bulldog will leap with excitement at any suggestion of a walk. When you first put a lead on an uninitiated puppy, try to avoid pulling on and dragging the puppy about as this will result in a panic attack and a bucking-bronco or catherine-wheel type display as the puppy is dragged along the floor or the drive. Instead, talk to him and encourage him to follow you. On your puppy's first walks you will be doing all the encouragement, but eventually, as he gains confidence, he will be the one trying to pull you! Here the voice is the most effective control: give a short sharp 'No' and a light tug, then as soon as he begins to walk alongside give soft-voiced praise. He will soon get the idea and trot along nicely.

Choke-chains are fine if used in moderation. The thin, metal, small-linked, show-type leads are fine for short stints in the show ring but are unsuitable for everyday road walking. They will act like wire around the neck and eventually will begin to break the fur.

Training Clubs

Most areas have dog training classes, which are normally held on weekday evenings in schools or village or community centre halls. The contact addresses are normally readily available from your nearest veterinary surgery. The chances are that few of the instructors will have any experience of Bulldogs, but once you have established yourself as a regular at least one of them will make an effort to ensure they know the show-ring procedure for standing and walking a Bulldog. Even if you have little or no inclination to embrace the showing side, ringcraft is a marvellous way for both you and your dog to meet, socialize, and exchange ideas and views with others.

Aim to start at these classes when your puppy is fourteen weeks old, but remember that he will be easily over-excited and quickly tired; aim for a gradual build-up to full adult training sessions.

5

Adolescent and Adult Management

Housing

Over the years I have formed mixed views with regard to housing Bull-dogs in kennels. In some respects, the dogs kept outdoors have been less prone to skin and respiratory problems, but the Bulldog is primarily a social animal, preferring the company of humans to that of other dogs, thriving on love, affection and creature comforts. For this reason, after their respective show or breeding careers are at an end, I immediately look for a suitable domestic home for the remainder of their days, rather than let them languish in a kennel.

Many breeds of dog are basically pack animals, perfectly happy with each other's company, whereas the Bulldog deteriorates without love and comfort. If you are going to the trouble of buying a Bulldog, it seems pointless then to keep him away from you in a kennel. This might not always apply if you are a serious breeder or exhibitor, but even so a Bulldog is not a guinea pig or rabbit, and outdoor housing is not something you can afford to get wrong. If you consider that a Bulldog is an expensive pedigree animal, it makes for false economy to construct a kennel from oddments of timber or orange boxes. All the weekly canine papers carry regular advertisements from experienced, reputable kennelling manufacturers, most of whom have countless years of experience, more often than not in your chosen breed.

I have found from past experience that outdoor kennelling must be of a height that allows you to walk in and out without banging your head. Low-roofed kennels are hazardous when you are constantly going back and forth and are extremely difficult to clean. Consult the professionals, who will advise on the correct structure, flooring and size runs. With brick or concrete kennels take particular care that the damp courses are adequate and are included in the flooring, and that the bases of the runs are well drained. Large puddles or constant wet areas will badly affect the dogs' feet, and in the summer they are breeding grounds for insects.

Remember that Bulldogs love chewing, something that never leaves them, and a thing that will be exacerbated when confronted with long boring stint in a kennel. Most of my beautiful state-of-the-art, cedar picture-postcard kennels have been reduced to matchstick wood within hours of occupancy, much to my despair. And Bulldogs would never win prizes at the Chelsea Flower Show: over decades we have ploughed a small fortune into shrubs, climbing roses, clematis, conifers, and ivies, and every carefully nurtured plant has become a nondescript stump.

It is of the utmost importance that not only for their physical health, but for their mental well-being, all kennel dogs are exercised on a regular basis.

Hygiene

Ask your breeder to recommend good disinfectants. Take care here, as some well-known products are extremely toxic, killing all known germs as well as practically everything else. It might also be a good idea to consider purchasing separate deodorizers, especially during the summer months, when bad smells happen fast and carry over large distances. Many of the old timers in dogs used to swear on good old-fashioned bleach. Most bleaches on today's market vary tremendously in strength and, if the run is constantly wet, can badly burn the dogs' feet. This in turn leads to splitting and cracking of the pads with the inevitable accompanying lameness.

A Brush with Success

Frequent brushing with either a medium (not harsh) bristle brush or, as I prefer, a rubber handglove, not only helps soften loose dead hair, improve circulation, and help to stimulate the release of natural oils into the dog's coat, but can become a fun and pleasurable experience for both Bulldog and owner. So much so, in fact, that many of my own dogs enjoy being vacuumed at intervals throughout the day while I tidy around the house.

A Bulldog's face should be cleaned religiously each day, without fail. Use tissue to remove any sleep from the eyes, and I find baby wipes, available from any high-street chemist, excellent for cleaning the creases. Your Bulldog will dislike this procedure, so try to make it as quick and entertaining for him as possible. It is imperative that it is done, and must become an absolute habit, much as it is for us to clean our teeth each morning.

The Nose

The nose must not be neglected as food deposits can build up under the crease and cause a bad odour, drying and cracking. A small dab of petroleum jelly is perfect for this. Sometimes the nose may crack and a small piece break off. This will prove to be sore and painful for your Bulldog but will eventually grow back, but pink in colour. This is not permanent and the pigment will eventually return although this will take many weeks, possibly months.

Ears

The Bulldog's rose-shaped ear, though neat and attractive, is also a warm breeding ground for mites. The ears must be checked regularly, both inside and out. Often owners complain of hair loss either on or around the rim of the ear. This is usually caused by microscopic mites and can be remedied by running benzyl benzoate around the rim of the outer ear with your finger.

Continued or excessive scratching and head shaking usually indicates inflammation, a sure sign either of a build-up of wax or the presence of ear mites. Wax should be carefully removed with a softening

agent, available from the vet or pet shop, using cotton wool. Cotton-wool buds are useful for cleaning between the creases of the inner ear flap but on no account should you delve too deeply into the ear anywhere near the ear canal. Here again I find cotton eye-wipes, meant for the removal of eye make-up, thinner and more suited for this task.

Champion bitch: Ch. Aldridge Anemone, owned by Les and Ellen Cotton. (Photo: The Bulldog Club Inc.)

If, having treated the ears for mites, your dog continues to scratch or shake his head, consult your vet.

Nails

Nails on a regularly exercised Bulldog need little, if any attention, although some Bulldogs have one or two nails that appear to stay longer than the others, probably as a result of the Bulldog's particular gait. One must also keep an eye on the dew-claws, which for some reason breeders are required to leave on. I personally find them to be a nuisance throughout the dog's life; they serve no purpose in the domestic dog and it would make sense to have them removed at birth. Many Bulldogs have a habit of jumping up and I am always worried that the dew-claws will get caught and tear away.

When clipping nails, keep in mind that speed is of the essence: dragging things out will only prove stressful to both you and the dog. Having said this, clipping nails quickly and efficiently takes some practice; so don't sacrifice accuracy for speed, just try to get the job done with as little fumbling and false starts as possible. To begin with, either the breeder or the vet will be happy to show you the ropes. I have got trimming nails to such a fine art that it is game-set-and-match before the dog realizes exactly what has happened.

Clip away just a small portion of the nail. With white nails you can see the pink blood vessels (quick) inside the nail. Take care not to cut too close to it as it will bleed very easily, sometimes profusely. Black nails are attractive, but you should take extra care here because the quick is not visible. Even when the nails are extremely long, do not clip away more than a small amount; within a few days the quick will withdraw further up the nail, enabling you to clip a little more nail away. In case of

Ch. Sandean Sophie's Baby, holder of the Bitch Breed Record during her lifetime, with her breeder/owner Terry Brunton.

93

any accidents it is a good idea to have a clotting agent such as permanganate of potash to hand: a little dabbed on the tip of the nail will
arrest bleeding. If you do cut the quick in any case, don't panic – the
bleeding looks worse than it is and seldom lasts for long.

One excellent way to wear down nails is to road-walk the dog in wet
weather, which softens the nails, enabling the nail to wear away faster.
The claws are made of keratin (like hair).

Bath Time

It is quite in order to bath your Bulldog, but do it infrequently. A dog's
skin is different from a human's, being very rich in oil glands and defi-
cient in sweat glands. The oil keeps the skin soft and prevents it from
drying and cracking. It also protects the coat and keeps it water resis-
tant. When a dog is bathed too often, the natural oil is removed from
the skin and this can result in dryness. Minute cracks in dry skin can
cause irritation, ultimately leading to redness or eczema.

When bathing is necessary, always ensure that everything is at hand
before placing your Bulldog in the bath. Towels, canine shampoo, and
an extra pair of hands if possible. Make sure that you have a thermo-
statically controlled shower, set at a temperature slightly higher than
lukewarm. Test this on a sensitive skin area such as that on the back of
your hands or inside arm.

1. Cover the floor with towels, ready for when you remove your dog
   from the bath. Then lift him carefully into the bath. If you have one,
   place a rubber mat in the bottom of the bath to prevent slipping.
2. Start by thoroughly soaking the body from the back of the neck,
   leaving out the head. Constantly talk and reassure your Bulldog
   and try to make this a pleasurable, not stressful experience.
3. When the coat is thoroughly wet, shampoo the neck and back, then
   the sides. Put the shower over once again before starting to work up
   a lather. Work downwards and underneath, shampooing through
   the front and back legs and feet, paying particular attention to the
   tail area. Rinse off thoroughly and then re-apply.
4. Tilt the head back and soak it with water applied with your hands. Take
   care to avoid any contact with the eyes. Apply the shampoo and work
   it in with your hands, massaging the head and wrinkles with care.
   Rinse the body until the water runs clear, leaving the head until last.
5. To rinse the head, tilt it back, covering the ears as you work your
   way down the sides. Make sure the creases are rinsed thoroughly

and quickly, preventing any water from entering the dog's eyes.

6. Finish rinsing, switch off the shower, and squeeze any excess water from the coat. Your Bulldog will probably vigorously shake any water from his coat, so be armed with a thick towel and be ready for a shower yourself.

7. Lift your Bulldog out of the bath and place him directly on to the towels on the floor. Under no circumstances should you let him climb or jump out. He could easily slip and badly damage himself.

8. First, towel-dry the head, making sure that the creases are thoroughly dry. Check inside the ears, again around the tail area, and in between the toes and under the pads. You can accelerate the process by using a hand-drier set at a moderate heat and low speed. With my hands I brush along, not against, the coat. This brings out a nice shine and bloom.

Many prefer vigorous brushing to bathing in preparation for a show on the grounds that bathing removes essential oils from the coat. I can appreciate this view and would certainly advocate bathing only in moderation, but no amount of localized 'dry' cleaning will remove the greasy feel and the odour from the coat. No matter how clean your Bulldog's coat may appear to be, you will be surprised to see how much dirt, dust and debris comes out when you rinse away the lather. Your Bulldog will look and feel and smell so much better!

Stepping into Summer

Excessive heat is dangerous for any breed of dog. Dogs can sweat only through their pads, and they reduce body heat by dispersing it through their body system by panting. Dogs are therefore very susceptible to heat stroke. Bulldogs enjoy the sun and warm weather, and I have often looked out on to the lawn to see a group of them basking like a shoal of beached whales. However, common sense is of the essence here. Exercise either early in the morning or late at night. As always, the answer is little and often. No-one in their right mind would consider taking their Bulldog for a ten-mile hike when the temperature is approaching 90 degrees in the shade.

If the weather is hot, take great care. Last summer I was told of a heartbroken owner who had gone for a light stroll in woodlands and lost her way. The hours of trekking proved too much of an ordeal and the dog died in the owner's arms. If there is no option but to walk your

Tugga Tough Decision for Kelloe, sire of five champions, sunbathing with his puppies.

dog at a given time, carefully plan a familiar route and if at all possible carry a phone in case backup is needed.

Never leave your dog alone in the car in summer. The clouds could part and the sun on the car raise the interior temperature to over-hot within minutes. Leaving the tailgate open is not a solution: it can slam shut.

Most Bulldogs enjoy travelling in cars but some, especially those of a nervous disposition, may stand and pant for the entire journey. If you can possibly afford it, air conditioning in the car is a godsend. If your dog starts to pant excessively, watch for the colour of the tongue, which should be a red pink, and listen to the breathing. If the dog appears to roar or the tongue turns blue, stop immediately and seek assistance. Don't be afraid to either pull into a garage or knock on a stranger's door – this is a matter of life and death and niceties can be exchanged later. The quickest way to reduce the body temperature is to totally immerse the dog in a cold bath, or, if that is not possible, to hose the dog with cold water. Bags of frozen peas or other packaged vegetables are also useful for assisting the drop in body temperature. If the dog is losing consciousness, ice-cubes placed against the rectum can help.

Once the dog appears to be on the mend, dry him and place him in a cool place where he can relax. Give him water to drink, but avoid administering excessive amounts as this could result in the bringing up of froth and the danger of choking. If your dog is prone to coughing up this type of thick white froth, it is a good idea to carry a squeezy bottle of lemon juice. Acidic citrus juice quickly helps to cut through the phlegm. Don't confuse this phlegm with the bright yellow froth that is usually bile from the stomach when the dog is unwell on an empty stomach. If your dog does not regain his normal body temperature (101.5°F/38.6°C) fairly quickly, you must take him to the vet as a matter of urgency. Heatstroke can be fatal very quickly. It is in any case a good idea to take a heatstroke victim to a vet, who will check him for shock (*see* Chapter 10). Shock is in itself a dangerous condition and frequently follows severe heatstroke.

Although the car is the most common place for a dog to be found with heatstroke, other environments can cause problems.

At summer shows where benching is placed under canvas, the lack of air circulation can lead to oppressive heat. Take plenty of towels that have been soaked in water, rolled up and placed in the freezer overnight. Fill sealable plastic containers with water and, again, freeze. Once the lid is removed it will melt gradually, providing iced drinking water throughout the day. There are numerous cold containers or cool bags on today's market, all easily carried when travelling.

Many canine product suppliers now provide cloth collars filled with crystals that, when immersed in water, swell and can then be frozen. These stay cold for hours and are easily placed around the Bulldog's neck, immediately reducing body temperature at the place where it counts – the blood-flow to the brain. Most army surplus stores now supply flat-pack polythene water containers resembling giant hot-water bottles that fit perfectly underneath the show cages. These should be frozen and towels placed between them and the cage.

My suggestions are not intended to panic bulldog owners, just to provide an insurance against the worst scenario. With careful planning and common sense, almost all disasters could be avoided.

The Elderly Bulldog

One of the most commonly asked questions is 'How long do Bulldogs live?' And I suppose the answer could be 'How long is a piece of string?' A good average would be around eight years, although I have known many to live into their teens. Such a one was Pauline Horner's champion bitch Honclo Sweet Clover, but Lesdor Lucky Number, whose brother was sold to film star Jayne Mansfield, is currently on record as the oldest Bulldog at sixteen and a half years. They were bred by Jack Cook by the renowned Tredgold Gaius Caligula.

The elderly Bulldog will need plenty of clean soft bedding, well away from any draughts, coupled with even more attention, love and assurance. As they grow old, many Bulldogs tend to lose their sight and care must be taken to avoid placing new obstacles about the house or reorganizing the furniture.

It is your responsibility to keep your dog alive for as long as he is happy and comfortable. You may well cope with debilitating illnesses, but when the rear quarters start to go wobbly to the point where rising up and out of bed whether to eat or to clean himself becomes a real effort, or if senile dementia sets in, then the time has come to make the decision as to whether you are being the selfish party by prolonging the suffering.

Euthanasia

Euthanasia is a quick and dignified end. It is always a difficult decision but, once you have made it, phone your vet and try to arrange a special appointment, out of normal surgery hours.

Most veterinary practices offer a cremation service, something that I personally prefer, but many find it comforting to take their bullies back home to be laid to rest in familiar surroundings.

Loved the Show, Loathed the Finale

It is the inevitable that we all dread and never care to mention but have to face up to sooner or later. No matter how many Bulldogs that you have at any one time, one dog never takes the place of another. Each Bulldog is a major part of your life, and his loss is something that you may find difficult to talk about amongst yourselves, let alone with complete strangers. Memories are everywhere, even in the sweeping over of the spot where he always lay. I once read the following quote, 'The Bulldog tears our hearts harder and a little earlier than other dogs, and we can only seek consolation in the reflection, "Whom the gods love, die young"'. Actually, Bulldogs are nowhere near as vulnerable as others would lead us to believe, and with proper treatment can be long-living hardy creatures.

6

Showing

Preparation for, Entry, Show Training, Presentation, Types of Show/Classes, Awards

Most people buy their first Bulldog as a pet but often, once the novelty of the new puppy begins to wear off, they become curious to know how good a specimen of the breed their dog is.

If you decide to try your dog in the show ring, you must be prepared to accept that you may travel for many hours and many miles only to have your dog unplaced when you get there. You may have great success at your first outing only to have your high hopes dashed at the next show. In short, one has to take the rough with the smooth. Some years ago I took my top champion dog to Crufts. He went Reserve in the Utility Group, beaten only by the dog that went on to become Reserve Supreme Champion. The following week I took the same dog to a breed championship show, only to have him placed fifth out of five in the Open Class. The dog was Champion Tyegarth Jacob of Kelloe, who lived to fight another day going Reserve Supreme Champion at Crufts four years later in 1986.

It is difficult to balance the competitive spirit possessed by most successful sportsmen with the feeling of being downhearted or annoyed at a low placing. The old adage has always been and always will be that you take home the same dog as the one you arrived at the show with. Showing brings out the best and the worst in all of us.

The Show Scene

The show scene appeals to many types of people from varying age groups and backgrounds. It attracts a complete cross-section of society, and the levelling factor is purely love of the Bulldog. All are equal in this game, with respect and deference paid to those with experience, knowledge and breeding and showing success. It is a sport in which you will make enemies as well as lifelong friends, and as a hobby it can be a consuming interest throughout a lifetime. Arthur Braithewaite of the Wyngrove affix was stewarding at shows right up into his nineties, and I have watched the likes of Kath Cook win CCs handling her own homebred dogs when she was well into her eighties. In more recent years, women in their late sixties and seventies, having successfully shown in other breeds for countless years, have entered the breed, showing, breeding and campaigning with some success.

Beginners have been known to have a meteoric start with an excellent dog, and are well and truly bitten by the show bug. Others, who may feel that their Bulldog has been placed unfairly, become disheartened and eventually drop out, and the drop-out rate is extremely high. Many enjoy the shows, win or lose, for what they are – an enjoyable day out. Others enter the spirit of showing with both feet first, embarking on the social mountaineering that they hope will carry them to the very top!

The best-learned lessons are the hard ones, and we can all recollect tales of heartbreak as well as those of elation. But I have always maintained that Bulldogs are one of the few breeds where if a novice has an exceptional dog and sticks with him, he will eventually rise to the surface. If they achieve this aim it is then that they learn that you can

Ch. Tyegarth Jacob of Kelloe owned by the author, winning Reserve Best in Show at Crufts 1986. Co-owner David McHale is handling. (Photo: Whitehouse.)

measure your popularity by the success you enjoy. One often hears the term 'a top person in the breed'. This can be misapplied to someone who has either bred a string of champions or whose stock is currently beating all comers in the ring. To my mind, a top person in any breed is one that has been involved at grassroots level for many years and has experienced virtually everything, good and bad, during that period.

Over the years dogs appear on the show scene that are referred to as 'flyers'. They rise steadily through the ranks and take a breed by storm. I have been fortunate to have two of these, Ch. Tyegarth Jacob of Kelloe and Ch. Kelloe White Glove. Some have left their mark and others have sunk without trace. A few, although leaving little in the way of stock, have nevertheless left a marked impression if only by altering breeders' and the public's attitude towards the breed.

In the case of Jacob, he was our third Bulldog and we were fairly new to the game. He won his first ticket at the Ladies' Kennel Association show in the Puppy Class under the breed's doyen, Dora Wakefield. Early on in the following year, Jacob was taking group and Best in Show awards. Jacob changed the public's perception of the Bulldog, previously considered somewhat dim and plodding. His extrovert, outgoing, energetic and unpredictable manner made him a great dog star of the 1980s, if not something of a liability in the show ring. On one occasion he tried to remove the Best in Show judge's toupée, ran amok with the late Joe Braddon's cap, and was seen trotting around the group ring with what appeared to be a full beard, but turned out to be half the Standard Poodle's tail plume in his mouth. At this time, Joe Braddon was the world's most accomplished and senior judge.

Some said Jacob was perfectly balanced, others that he excelled in nothing. At the end of the day he notched up thirty-four CCs, eight Utility Groups, three Best in Shows (at Welsh Kennel Club, West of England Ladies' Kennel Club (WELKS), and Windsor) and four Reserve Best in Shows. Jacob lived to be eleven years old. I will always remember the day he died. We were sitting in the kitchen, the back door flew open with a tremendous bang, Jacob stood with a slight sway, astride the lintel. He looked straight through us, then turned away and made for his bed. He had come to say goodbye.

Ch. Kelloe White Glove, on the other hand, took some time before she began winning tickets. Minnie, as she was known at home, eventually got her break, winning a first ticket, with the Best of Breed at WELKS under Sheena Haydock, and that day went on to Reserve in the group. The group judge that day was a Maharajah! She made up to a champion in the following three straight shows. She not only took

Ch. Kelloe White Glove, the Breed Record holder with 50 CCs all won under different judges. 'Minnie' was bred by the author and David McHale. (Photo: Pearce.)

the Bitch CC Breed Record, held throughout her lifetime by Terry Brunton's beautiful Ch. Sandean Sophie's Baby, but eventually overtook the Dog CC Breed Record, held since the mid-1970s by Dennis Shaw's top-winning dog Ch. Beechlyn Golden Nugget of Denbrough. Minnie's fiftieth CC came at Richmond in 1995 under breed specialist Jean Booth, and she was retired on the day.

With White Glove, the tally of tickets was really more of a progression than a conscious effort. It rapidly got to the stage where people were telling us that we were only three CCs away from the bitch record. Next thing we knew, the list was reaching the forty mark and, as she was still so young and in full bloom it made sense to 'go for it'. In hindsight, it is something I would never consider doing again. Although it has been great fun, it was also a stressful time.

Types of Show

Showing is a useful means of monitoring whatever direction we are moving in as breeders. Shows are initially the saviour of the breed and are vitally important as they maintain the Standard. Without them, the breed would lose direction as people would gradually begin to breed indiscriminately.

There are various types of show, starting with the Exemption Show, through Limit, Open and Championship Shows, and finishing at the top with general Championship Shows.

Ch. Ocobo Skipper, owned and bred by Pat and Norman Davis. (Photo: The Bulldog Club Inc.)

Ch. Aldridge Advent Gold, owned by Les and Ellen Cotton. (Photo: The Bulldog Club Inc.)

Exemption Shows

Exemption shows are so called because they are exempt from Kennel Club Rules, which means that they can be entered by pedigree dogs and family 'Heinz-57' pets alike. They will be advertised in the canine press, such as *Dog World* or *Our Dogs*, or in the local papers. There will be novelty as well as pedigree classes but these will inevitably be mixed breeds and sexes. You will be expected just to go along, make yourself known to the secretary or steward, and enter on the day. Exemption shows are good practice and a light-hearted start to the show scene.

Limit Shows

These are for dogs that have not yet won a Challenge Certificate, and they are sometimes limited to club members, hence the name. Limit Shows can take the form of breed or all-breed shows. To enter, you need to contact the club or breed-club secretary, who will post you a schedule. These are usually sent automatically to club members.

Matches

The British show scene has some twenty Bulldog breed clubs,

Ch. Beechlyn Golden Nugget of Denborough, bred by Joe Fox and owned by Dennis and Barbara Shaw. A prominent winner of the 1970s. (Photo: Pearce.)

many of which hold annual puppy competitions. These are generally light-hearted social events which are normally held under the Match system, in which dogs compete on a knockout basis. The dogs are assessed by three judges of mixed ability and experience. Under current Kennel Club rules, any puppy that has previously won a Challenge Certificate is ineligible to compete in matches. This, to my mind is senseless as it precludes the best puppies in the country from competing!

Open Shows

As the name implies, open shows are open to all – first-timers and champions alike. They are for one breed only or for all breeds. Even though Challenge Certificates are not on offer, the competition can be very strong, and many open shows held by premier clubs often attract larger entries than the breed classes laid on at some of the general championship shows.

The Bulldog of the Year show is an example of this where the CC-winners' class for the title of Bulldog of the Year is class 17 of the club's morning open show. As with the limit shows, you will need to contact the secretary well in advance and apply for a schedule.

Championship Shows

This is the top of the show tree, and the place where Challenge Certificates are awarded.   Championship shows can take the form of either an individual breed

The author handling Ch. Tyegarth Lucifer after winning the Utility Group and Reserve Best in Show at Windsor Championship Show 1983. The Judge is Sigurd Wilburg, and the award is presented by Her Serene Highness The Princess Antoinette of Monaco. Lucifer was then exported to Sweden where he died tragically in a fire at the home of the famous judge and French Bulldog breeder Ulla Segerstrom. (Photo: Hartley.)

104

club show or a general (all-breed) championship show where all breeds are scheduled. Always check to see if Bulldogs have been allocated Challenge Certificates at each particular show as there are often classes for Bulldogs that do not offer CCs. At the end of judging the best dog will come up against the best bitch for the judge to choose Best of Breed. The winner of Best of Breed will then be entitled to represent that breed in the group judging (in the case of Bulldogs, the Utility Group), regardless of whether CCs were on offer or not.

The winner of the group is then entitled to go forward to compete for Best in Show. At a Bulldog Breed Club Championship Show the best dog and bitch compete at the end of the show for the Best in Show award. This is then followed by the Best Puppy award, unless the best puppy has just won the Best in Show.

Classes

Dogs are entered in classes put on for their respective ages, some taking into account previous wins. A puppy's age must be calculated from the first day of the show, so take care to account for this when filling in the form. With these provisos the following are the definitions of the main classes, which are normally printed inside the show schedules.

Minor Puppy For dogs of six and not exceeding nine calendar months of age on the first day of the show.
Puppy For dogs of six and not exceeding twelve calendar months on the first day of the show.
Junior For dogs of six and not exceeding eighteen calendar months on the first day of the show.
Maiden For dogs which have not won a Challenge Certificate or a first prize at an open or championship show (Minor Puppy, Special Minor Puppy, Puppy and Special Puppy classes excepted, whether restricted or not).
Special Yearling For dogs of twelve and not exceeding twenty-four months of age on the first day of the show.
Undergraduate For dogs which have not won a Challenge Certificate or three or more first prizes at championship shows (Minor Puppy, Special Minor, Puppy and Special Puppy classes excepted, whether restricted or not).
Graduate For dogs which have not won a Challenge Certificate or four or more first prizes at championship shows in Graduate, Post

Graduate, Minor Limit, Mid-Limit, Limit, and Open classes, whether restricted or not.

Post-Graduate For dogs which have not won a Challenge Certificate or five or more first prizes at championship shows in Post-Graduate, Minor Limit, Mid-Limit, and Open classes, whether restricted or not.

Limit For dogs which have not won three Challenge Certificates under three different judges or seven or more first prizes in all at championship shows in Limit and Open classes, confined to the breed, whether restricted or not, at shows where Challenge Certificates were offered for the breed.

Open For all dogs of the breed eligible for entry at the show (including champions).

In the United Kingdom, all puppies must be over the calendar age of six months, whereas overseas many show societies put on young puppy classes for those of twelve weeks to five months old. These are in the main fun classes with no titles or awards on offer, the judge being asked just to give an opinion and a grading of 'Promising' or 'Very Promising'.

The Main Events

Three of the biggest highlights of the breed's show calendar are Crufts, and two events organized by the Bulldog Club Incorporated, namely Bulldog of the Year and the Bulldog Club Championship Show.

Crufts

Many feel that Crufts is not particularly large in terms of entries when compared to some

Ch. Willsmere Solid Silver, owned and bred by Graham and Viv Williams, four times Bulldog of the Year and Best of Breed at Crufts in 1992. (Photo: The Bulldog Club Inc.)

Carol Newman (Wencar Bulldogs) shakes hands with HRH Prince Michael of Kent, patron of Crufts. (Photo: Marc Henrie.)

other shows on the circuit, and it is just another championship show but, when all is said and done, Crufts is the show that the world watches. It is the one championship show that your Bulldog has to qualify for, usually by winning a first, second or third placing in certain classes at a previous championship show. This is also the show where you seldom bump into a close pal or neighbour but may well meet a long-lost friend from the other side of the globe.

Crufts is the show sometimes referred to as the top dog's graveyard, and during the time that I have been showing I have known at least two Bulldogs beat several well-established champions to win their first ever Challenge Certificate with Best of Breed Crufts, and then never win another.

I have often been asked exactly what it was like to be on the rostrum with the famous Jacob after winning Reserve Supreme Champion in 1986. All I can remember is the television cameras, flashbulbs popping, and people congratulating us. In the Utility Group judging, Jacob (as always the extrovert) had jumped up and grabbed the rosette from the group judge Joe Braddon's hand. For many, this proved to be one of the best parts of the show, and in the final line-up for Supreme Champion the Reserve rosette was again unceremoniously snatched form the hands of the then Kennel Club chairman, the late John McDougall. This met with a fanfare from the press and Jacob received more media coverage than the outright winner! Di Johnson, herself breeder of a Crufts group winner and a noted writer, described Jacob as 'probably the most personality-plus dog of our era'; and Joe Braddon, who at the time was the only judge in the world qualified to award Challenge Certificates in every breed, later said in a television interview, that in his view Bulldogs of Jacob's ilk were so few and far between that he should have won Supreme Champion!

Bulldog of the Year

Bulldog of the Year was first held in 1977. Entrance is by invitation only, and each contestant must have won at least one CC during the preceding year. The three judges place the dogs in complete secrecy; none of them confer. The four finalists are announced at the end of the contest in reverse order, as all the contestants are considered winners in their own right.

Three of the first five winners of the titles were bitches. However, no bitch has taken the title since Ch. Merriveen Maybe Baby in 1981. It has been won by Ch. Willsmere Solid Silver on four occasions, and the Outdoors kennel of Brian Daws and Dora Wakefield is the only one to have won Bulldog of the Year with three different homebred dogs: Ch. Outdoors Jubilant (1978); Ch. Outdoors Jubi Junior (1979); Ch. Outdoors Country Gent (1995). The kennel is also the first and only one to have won both titles in one year (1995) – Ch. Outdoors Country Gent (Bulldog of the Year), and Ch. Kentee Kizzy at Outdoors (winner of the Bulldog Club Championship Show).

Challenge Certificates

Challenge Certificates (CCs, or 'tickets' as they are sometimes referred to) are the green and white cards presented to the best of the line-up of class winners of each sex at a championship show. A dog must win three Challenge Certificates (CCs) under three different judges to become a champion. At least one of the CCs must be won after the dog is one year of age. I remember watching the famous Ch. Outdoors Jubi Junior, who took numerous tickets while a puppy, win a crowning CC at a little over a year old.

The title of champion is the ultimate award for any dog and the one to which every exhibitor aspires. Once acquired, the title is confirmed in writing with a certificate from the Kennel Club. It can never be taken away, no matter how often that particular dog is beaten in competitions, and it also means lifelong qualification for Crufts.

A dog can carry on showing and winning CCs for as many years as the owner wishes. Some feel that after a dog has attained his title, often referred to as 'made up', he should be retired to allow others to do the same. Many believe that three CCs and 'one for luck' make the dog a true champion and not just a fluke. There is the train of thought that a top-flight winning dog stops others from attaining their titles. This can often be the case, but then all dogs are there at the show to be beaten. The reason that most often they are not ensures that the high standards within the breed are maintained. I have seen some very unremarkable champions, some of which I consider were made up by default or merely for attendance!

Showing in the Republic of Ireland

The Republic of Eire has its own separate canine administration, the Irish Kennel Club (IKC). This operates a totally different system from the UK's. All dogs, including British ones, have to be registered with the IKC to be allowed to enter and exhibit on the Irish show circuit.

Green Stars

Awards made in the Republic of Ireland that count towards the title of champion are known as Green Stars. Each Green Star is worth a certain number of points, and fifteen points are needed to become a champion. The number of points awarded with each Green Star depends on factors such as the number of dogs entered and also those actually present on the day. As with our system of Reserve Challenge Certificates, Reserve Green Stars are awarded in case the Green Star winner is later disqualified for any reason.

Dos Aguas Konrad, CAC winner at Murcia Championship Show 1997.

Italy's leading breeders, and no newcomers to top honours, Chiara Guria (left) handling All To Love Sonny Jnr, and Paolo Bonnetto (right) with Luky Line di Hawkroad. The judge (centre) is Antonio di Lorenzo.

Showing in Europe

The Fédération Cynologique Internationale is the controlling body for most of the European shows and breeders. At FCI shows, each dog is judged individually and given a written critique before leaving the ring. The judge is also required to grade each exhibit:

Excellent. A Bulldog that fits the Breed Standard.

Very Good. A Bulldog with some minor faults but still considered suitable for breeding.

Good. A Bulldog that is not typical of the breed and should not be bred from. In some countries, three such awards would mean breeding is prohibited.

There are two types of FCI shows: international shows at which CACIBs (Certificat d'Aptitude Championat International de Beauté) are awarded, and national shows at which CACs (Certificat d'Aptitude au Championat) are awarded. These certificates are the equivalents of the Kennel Club's Challenge Certificate. Puppies are not allowed to win CACs or Reserve CACs, but are allowed to compete at the end of judging for the Best of Breed.

Ch. Dos Aguas Jacob, a grandson, maternally and paternally, of the celebrated Jacob of Kelloe. A champion of Spain, Portugal and international champion, Jacob was Bulldog of the Year in Spain for 1995 and 1996, and Top Stud-Dog 1997. This highly successful kennel, Dos Aguas, is the partnership of Peter Frantzen and his wife Porn Maimon.

National and International Titles

Rules for becoming a national champion differ in each European country. In Scandinavia, for example, a Bulldog cannot become a full champion until he has passed temperament tests, designed to prove that he is mentally stable.

The title of International Champion is something of a rarity in the United Kingdom because draconian quarantine laws make it difficult for British dogs to compete in FCI countries. There are moves being made to relax the quarantine laws – after all, six months in the life of a Bulldog is the equivalent of three-and-a-half years of solitary confinement in human terms. The sensible way forward appears to be vaccination, using tattooing, micro-chipping and pets' passports as means of identifying vaccinated dogs.

To become an international champion, a dog must win four CACIBs in three different countries, and two of these must be won in their country of residence. All the CACIBs must be won under different judges.

Showing in the USA

As well as having their own Standard, the Americans have a totally different show system, with each sex being judged separately in the following classes:

Puppies. Six to nine months of age.
Puppies. Nine to twelve months of age.
Novice Class. For dogs who have never won a first prize in an adult class.
Exhibitor Bred. All Bulldogs six months or over (except champions), who are exhibited by the owner or partnership, and bred by them.

USA Bred. All Bulldogs bred in the USA (except champions).
Open Class. All Bulldogs over six months, including champions and imports, but most USA champions are shown in the special class.
Special Class. American champions.

The United States' system is similar to the Irish Kennel Club's, but instead of Green Stars, the awards are known as Winners 'Bitch' and Winners 'Dog', with the corresponding reserves.

Dogs are entered in only one class, and at the end of judging all unbeaten dogs are called back into the ring to compete for the title of Winners Dog and Winners Bitch. It is only the winners of these titles that are awarded points.

Any Bulldog that accumulates fifteen points becomes a Champion of Record with the American Kennel Club. The amount of points on offer at each show depends on how many Bulldogs of the same sex the winner has defeated in the class, and may also vary according to geographical region; there is a minimum of one point and a maximum of five. The fifteen accumulated points must include at least two shows with a minimum of three points (major show) under two different judges, and some of the remaining points must be under a third judge. When a Bulldog gains enough points and majors to qualify for his American Champion title, he is said to be 'finished'.

In American Kennel Club (AKC) shows, champions of record do not compete for the championship points. Instead, they join the Winners Dog and Winner Bitch to compete for the title Best of Breeds.

Westminster Dog Show

This is the most prestigious all-breed dog show in the United States – the equivalent of the British Crufts, the Italian Milan, the Spanish Madrid and the French Chantilly. The show is held annually each February in New York City. It is considered a very political show, limited to 2,500 dogs, all of which must be AKC champions of record. This limit is normally reached within two hours on the day on which the show superintendent accepts entries. The 1998 Bulldog entry was a total of eleven dogs.

Bulldog Club of America Nationals Week

The Bulldog of America (BCA) National Specialty Show takes place over three days of what has become a full week of Bulldog activities. The event is scheduled between 1 September and the end of the year, and rotates geographically around the USA. The 1997 Specialty, the largest ever, attracted over 500 Bulldogs.

In addition to the National Show, there are two back-up shows, which allow for three full sets of winners during the week. Competition includes the BCA National Sweepstakes, an Obedience Trial and Junior Showmanship. Other activities include the National Council Annual Meeting, educational seminars, a judge's workshop, display of the BCA National Gallery of Winners, the BCA Hall of Fame, and a BCA National Awards Banquet. Hundreds of Bulldoggers worldwide travel to this wonderful gathering each year.

Show Training

With every champion I have owned, or for that matter seen, however worthy, there has always been something about them that I would like to alter. All dogs have faults and virtues to a lesser or greater extent, and it is up to you as the handler to accentuate the good and minimize the not so good when exhibiting.

Show training can be a time-consuming and sometimes boring procedure for both parties concerned. For this reason, it is only natural to put the whole thing off, always finding some reason not to do it. However, your dedication and hard work will pay off for both of you when, at your first outing, you are conspicuous for your professionalism, and not for the misbehaviour that did not allow the judge to go over or properly assess your Bulldog.

Some Bulldogs are hyperactive, and will summon all your patience and self-control. Others are lazy and plodding. With the latter type, either a squeaky toy, concealed in your pocket, or perhaps a titbit such as baked liver will help to attract or encourage his attention.

Always be firm in your actions and in your voice tone, and impress upon your puppy that this is work not play! Be in control and, most importantly (especially with an unruly or difficult pupil) finish with yourself in charge. Never stop the training sessions in chaos, no matter how long it takes; always, without exception be in total control. Then relax and shower him with praise.

Ringcraft

Ringcraft classes are essential for the discipline and socialization of the potential show puppy, but it is doubtful whether there will be any instructors at your local classes who are familiar with the correct procedure for presenting a Bulldog.

In the show ring, you will be expected to 'stack' your Bulldog, that is, stand him still in a four-square position for several minutes at a time as the judge assesses his balance and conformation. The Bulldog must be stacked front on to the judge, rather than side on, so that the judge is able to look through the front legs and see the hind legs between them. This is probably the only breed that is required to present a front profile. In the United States, Bulldogs are presented side on in the more conventional manner. The dog will then be expected to allow the judge to 'go over' him to check his barrel of rib, check that he is entire, and to open and look inside his mouth.

You will then be asked to walk your dog in a reasonable-sized triangle, and then directly up and down in a straight line, and your dog should be able to do this in a free manner, on loose lead, neither pulling nor dragging. As you become more familiar with ring procedure and your dog's particular gait or movement, you will be able to identify the optimum speed at which to move him.

Start to practise stacking your puppy from around eight to ten weeks of age. You should use a steady, secure surface, and repeat the lesson almost daily if possible. By doing this, you will lay the foundations for a lifetime's discipline in the ring.

Always place a nylon show lead around his neck. Then place his front in the correct position by turning his pasterns inwards from the shoulder, not from the feet or pasterns. Cup your puppy's underjaw in the fingers of the hand holding the lead, and with the other ensure that his hind legs are positioned correctly to show off his hind angulation to advantage: neither way out behind, like a German shepherd, nor directly underneath, which will make him look stilted and straight behind.

Some Bulldogs – usually those of excellent conformation – will lean forward in the show ring, putting their whole body out of kilter. They will appear to go out at the shoulder, look low to the ground, and display their hindquarters at virtual right angles to their topline. This is so frustrating and it will take all your might to hold them back. You will recognize this stance because if you were suddenly to take your arm away your Bulldog would collapse in a heap. I find the best solution is to hold the front tightly with my thumb and forefingers on the centre of the breast-plate. This will soon become uncomfortable for your Bulldog and with calm reassuring words, he will begin to relax and rise up backwards.

Handling in the USA

Owing to the immense size of the country, and the vast areas that must be covered between shows, it is quite common for Bulldogs to have professional handlers. These tour the show scene in air-conditioned, purpose-built motor homes, often with an array of Bulldogs all placed in their charge for showing. The technique for presenting Bulldogs is quite different from that used in the United Kingdom. The Bulldog is stacked, mostly on his sides as opposed to head on, and the lead is pulled up and forward to emphasize the arch and reach of the neck, a little like the technique when showing terriers in the UK.

Entering Shows

All puppies, by virtue of their differing parentage and bloodlines, mature at different ages. This is where the help of your puppy's breeder will be of paramount importance: nobody will know their own lines better than they. In the United Kingdom, the Kennel Club require puppies to be six months old, on the first day of the show, before they can be exhibited at licensed events. Naturally, it will be difficult to resist the temptation to enter your Bulldog at the first available show. But experienced breeders or exhibitors often hold back young dogs that they may feel are not as yet ready for the show ring.

When filling in the entry forms and perusing the category of classes, bear in mind that your puppy may have matured, almost to adult size, by the age of six months. In this case it would be well worth while consulting with someone experienced and considering the possibility of entering him in a higher class, such as Puppy Dog or Junior Dog, rather than skipping Minor Puppy. In any event your first show, win or lose, will be an exciting and memorable experience.

As a newcomer you will probably be unfamiliar with the judges whose names are printed in the show schedules and will have to take your chances. In time you will become more discerning, recognizing the judges whose opinions are especially respected or those most likely to appreciate your particular type of Bulldog.

Schedules

A list of the number and type of class will be included with the entry form, along with the criteria for entry in each class. The UK is one of the few countries where a puppy can be entered in every class (except Veteran) and can compete for the Challenge Certificate or Best of Breed. FCI countries insist that dogs are entered in their age classification. I have often been frustrated when judging overseas when I have not been able to give the equivalent of the CC to the best dog purely because of his age. To my mind none of this makes sense, but when in Rome! I have often had no option but to pass the CC to an inferior dog, as of right, only to award Best of Breed to a younger and better exhibit.

Preparation

Preparation for your first show outing should be well in hand the previous day. If you plan to bath your Bulldog, make sure that this is done when you have time to do it properly (*see* Chapter 5). Any dampness will result in messy creases and movement could be affected by consequent cramp.

Make sure that you have studied the detailed information regarding the show venue, normally printed inside the schedules. It is no good waking up on the morning of the show, putting the dog in the car, wrapping your sandwiches in a map, and setting off, hoping for the best. Contact the main motoring associations, study the route that you intend to take, and bear in mind the difficulties that you may expect in certain areas at particular times of day. Always allow plenty of time, not only for the journey but for the walk from the car park: getting yourself, your dog, and all the bags to the hall or marquee where the Bulldogs are benched can take longer than you imagine. Breed championship venues will have adjoining car parks, but I have known all-breed championship shows where the Bulldog ring was a good twenty-minute stroll from the exhibitors' car park. Also be aware of the fact that if all judging is to commence at the same time (normally around ten o'clock) there will possibly be hundreds of owners as well as exhibits all arriving at the same time.

It is also a good idea to note whether there is a specified removal time, as it is called. Many show societies will stipulate that dogs entered at the shows have to remain on the site until a certain time.

This is to ensure that once dogs have been shown there is not a mass exodus from the show ground or venue, and that the public, who have paid a fee to enter the show as spectators, will have something to look at, if only the dogs on the benches.

What to Wear

Plan your outfit to complement your Bulldog. You will be expected to look reasonably professional without distracting attention from the exhibit. Women should avoid long flowing skirts that could flap around and detract from the general outline of the dog on the move and it is always wise to leave high heels and loose, dangling jewellery at home. Loose trousers and flat shoes appear to be the most widely accepted, sensible solution here.

De rigueur for male professional handlers has always been a shirt, tie and jacket. There may be prolonged spells, especially if it is a well-filled class, where you will be required to kneel for lengthy spells. Ensure that trousers are loose fitting enough to allow you to get down and stack your Bulldog, and that jackets are not too tight across the shoulders, restricting your arms when you reach over the dog.

A long wait at the dog show! (Photo: Simon Lathan.)

What to Take

Naturally you must take yourself and the right dog. This is not a flippant remark: I have known several kennels over the years who have inadvertently entered or taken the wrong exhibit to a show. Check the passes sent by the canine society the night before making sure not only that the right dog has been entered but also that he has been put into the right class. If you are going to a general championship or open show where other breeds will be scheduled, make sure that you know at approximately what time Bulldogs will be in the ring. Quite often there will be two or three breeds using the same judging ring in succession.

Along with your passes, you will need to take the schedule, the car-park ticket, and the ring cards for each individual dog. Kennel Club rules require handlers to display the dog's individual number at all times when he is in the ring, and this is usually the same as the benching number. If separate passes are issued, the gate stewards will normally request these later in the day when you leave the show. This is a precaution against wrongful taking or removal of dogs. You may also want to take your Bulldog's foldable cage, which will provide a secure place for him to rest between classes. I normally carry a grooming or show bag (usually termed a 'breed bag') for a few other necessities.

Breed Bags
Your breed bag should have a secure, separate pocket in which to keep the show schedule, the car-park ticket, and passes and ring cards as appropriate.

The contents of your individual breed bag will differ slightly with the time of the year. At all times, your bag will contain a bowl for drinking water, with an accompanying metal holder that clips

Ch. Ocobo Tully, owned and bred by Pat Davis. (Photo: The Bulldog Club Inc.)

on to the inside of the cage, dry towels, and a brush (I prefer the rubber hand-glove to the conventional brush, but you must ensure these are washed after each show). A chamois leather brings up a good bloom on the finished coat, and soft and hard grooming chalk, though not approved by the Kennel Club, is nonetheless to be found in almost every breed bag. I carry two plastic hand-sprays, one containing water for lightly spraying down the dog on hot or warm sultry days, and another containing diluted shampoo. Quite often the show ground will be either dusty or, in wet spells, muddy. A quick sprucing up and a rub down with a towel will restore the coat to its former glory. Other grooming items to include are cotton-wool balls and cotton-wool buds, petroleum jelly to soften cracked pads and dry noses, nail clippers (I prefer the guillotine type), and a pair of scissors to trim away loose untidy hairs.

In addition to your grooming kit, take travel sickness tablets for your Bulldog, a bottle-opener (for obvious reasons), a selection of show leads, a foldable umbrella or plastic raincoat or anorak, and a show clip in order to display your ring card. A lock and key will be useful so that you an secure your dog in his cage if you need to leave him for short periods, although it is advisable to ask another nearby exhibitor to keep an eye on your dog for you. Be prepared for a few accidents in the cage and take plenty of disposable kitchen towels. Lastly, if you are going to a show on your own, a trolley, available from trade stands at the larger general shows, will be an invaluable help and avoid countless trips back and forth to the car park.

For summer shows there are additional essentials: a thermal container for frozen drinking water, and soaked and frozen towels for cooling (*see* Chapter 5); a small plastic bottle of squeezed lemon (readily available on the market for cooking purposes) can be indispensable when confronted with a heat-distressed Bulldog as it cuts through froth, phlegm or bile.

In the Ring

Keep a close eye on the ringside and be prepared for the ring steward to call out firstly the class number and then the number of each exhibit. Give yourself plenty of time. If you are late and miss your class, you may not be able to enter any of the other breed classes scheduled for that day. Even if it is the only class in which the dog is entered, it may not be possible to have the dog transferred to any other class. If you have not been sent a numbered card by the show society, this will be

Bulldogs have a sense of humour. (Photo: Simon Lathan.)

handed to you by the steward as you enter the ring. When showing overseas, these cards are handed out by the stewards in numerical order and exhibitors are expected to take their place in the ring in this order. Here in the United Kingdom it is acceptable to place your dog in any position you please, within the confines of the line-up. I would advise the first-timer to avoid being the first to be seen. Try to place yourself somewhere in the middle, where you can watch the other exhibitors and give yourself time to get into your stride. It is also a mistake to be the last: you will not have the experience to get back into the line-up and place your dog for the judge's final perusal.

Aim to be calm, confident and relaxed. There is a train of thought that maintains that nervousness travels down the lead to the dog. The object is to make the entire exercise enjoyable and to finish with attention and lots of praise. The ringside will appreciate and admire a well-behaved dog but, at the other extreme, some kennels have become known for their over-handled, bored-looking and inanimate exhibits. As with other things in life, some people are natural handlers, quickly forming a rapport with whichever dog they take into the ring; others, no matter how hard they try, never quite achieve this and make the whole exercise appear laboured. My great friend Carl Johnson, renowned Dicarl Great Dane Breeder and handler, maintains that 'Good handlers make mediocre dogs look good, and make good dogs look great. But it is great dogs that make handlers.'

Use show leads of the loose-fitting nylon variety that fall away from the neck. Some prefer the fine-metal linked check type, but if your dog is lively and quite active, these could pull extremely tight when the dog is on the move, acting like cheese wire, tightly gripping the windpipe and eventually breaking the hair on the back of the neck. Do not make the cardinal mistake of 'stringing up' your Bulldog like a terrier. A good reach of neck is important, but there is no need to stretch him like a giraffe.

Keep an eye on both judge and exhibit. Look relaxed, be professional; never overhandle your dog. Many do this 'eyeballing', either to attract attention or unnerve the judge. Having said this, you can inconspicuously draw the judge's attention to your exhibit's good points. A gentle stroke along the back can accentuate a beautiful topline; but this can work the other way if a fidget or an unruly leg or pastern suddenly becomes apparent just as the judge makes a final assessment.

It is perfectly in order to be pleasant to the judge as he or she goes over your Bulldog, but it is considered bad form to carry on any lengthy conversations. In the lower classes the judge will probably ask the age of the dog, tell you where to stand, and then ask you to walk your Bulldog so as to assess his movement. When all the exhibits have been seen, you will be placed. There are normally five places, each accompanied by a card or rosette:

First. A red card or rosette.
Second. Blue card or rosette.
Third. Yellow card or rosette.
Fourth. Green card or rosette.
Very Highly Recommended (VHC). White card or rosette.

The Challenge Certificates, issued by the Kennel Club, are always the customary dark green and white. The Reserve CC cards are a smaller version, in green and white, while the Best of Breed cards are in an equally distinctive red and white.

In Europe, the colours of the placings differ from country to country, but blue is usually for first, with red given to the second placing. Coloured ribbons in the respective winning colours are handed out and exhibitors tie these onto their Bulldog's show leads.

In Conclusion

There is nothing better than the beaming smile of an excited winning exhibitor, but there is nothing worse than a disgruntled loser calling the judge all and sundry. Try to keep your opinions, however valid, to yourself and those closest to you. Act in haste and repent at leisure. Any comments will be frowned upon, so far better to postpone the post mortem on the day's events until the journey home in the car. Remember, as with all things in life, there are three points of view: theirs, yours and the truth!

7

Judging

Sidney H. Deacon once wrote:

> When one comes to think about it, it is surprising that in such a pastime as dog showing there are not more differences. It is not like a race or cricket match, where there is no doubt as to the absolute winner. The whole fabric of dog showing rests on the opinion of one man at each particular show, and most exhibitors look upon their own dog as the apple of their eye.

For my own part, becoming a judge was more of a progression than a conscious effort. Most of my formative years in Bulldogs were spent showing, handling and breeding, and though I was offered appointments I had no inclination to judge until my partner began to judge classes at

The author (centre) judging at The Bundeseiger Championship Show, Dortmund, Germany. One of Germany's top breeders, Petra Grell (left) handles her homebred Int. Ch. Simplissimus Bridget Bardot, with Imelda Anghern (right) handling her homebred Ch. Pickwick Quasimodo. Imelda and Evelyn Landis (Goldengrove Bulldogs) are the leading Swiss Bulldog breeders.

open shows, and then I too began to take an interest. I went straight in at the deep end, with my first appointment at a breed-club open show. When the appointment was offered, I was deeply flattered and accepted on the spot, but when the fateful day arrived and I had to queue for fifteen minutes to get into the car park I realized the enormity of the whole affair. The half-dozen dogs that were to be my launching pad turned into an entry of seventy, and I arrived to find a packed ringside and many of the breed's championship show judges and stalwarts, such as Minnie Wearmouth, Kath and Jack Cook, perched behind the judging table.

Like most judges, I remember that first appointment clearly. The first Bulldog entering the ring in Minor Puppy, his first show, was my eventual Best in Show, and I remember thinking that he had terrific bone and substance but couldn't afford to grow a centimetre. He went on to become Champion Merriveen McClean of Bullzaye, bred by Pat Dellar, and handled that day by a championship show judge, the late Betty Cassidy.

Why Judge?

A judging appointment is conferred as an honour, not as a right. Some consider it their lives' work to achieve this aim, and so they plough forward with almost indecent haste, while others often feel that it is a taxing experience that will make them unpopular and have no aspirations at all in this direction. Many believe that becoming a judge will give them impetus within a breed, whereas often their lack of judgement and indifferent placings will in fact have the opposite effect. Others may consider that an impending appointment will earn them celebrity status among their peers. But while many hopeful exhibitors may lay on the charm with a trowel, some will feel uncomfortable and even avoid the judge, who is probably a good friend, for weeks before the show.

Ch. Merriveen McClean of Bullzaye.
(Photo: The Bulldog Club Inc.)

The name of the game is never to ask for an appointment, but wait patiently until your aptitude and ability are noticed by others and you are approached by a club or society. Let your track record speak for itself. Remember, when the day finally arrives, that while you are judging the dogs, the ringside will be judging you.

Of course, there are odd judges who consider their appointment to be an opportunity to reward those who have done their stock well on previous occasions, and there are those who stand in the middle of the ring and hand out prizes quite indiscriminately. Many times one hears of those who stand for committees especially to gain an appointment, and others that have turned up at clubs' AGMs with the world and his wife as voters to achieve the same end.

However, such tactics are rarely successful in the long run. Those who eventually attain the status of knowledgeable, respected breed specialists are those who are considered fair, impartial people of integrity, not those who just carry a veneer of respectability.

Remember, first-time judges usually attract large entries as they are an unknown quantity, and many exhibitors, being curious, will give you the benefit of the doubt. But after the first flush, poor judges quickly acquire a reputation as such and their entries dwindle.

Responsibility

Judging carries a great deal of responsibility and so you must decide whether you feel that you have the strength of character to withstand the criticisms and resentments that will undoubtedly be levelled against you. The winners will naturally be delighted that you have confirmed their belief in the quality of their dogs, but equally the losers will be very disappointed that you have not fully appreciated the quality of their dogs, whom they obviously believe to be every bit as good (if not better) otherwise they wouldn't have been there in the first place.

You must also consider that as you accept more appointments, your opinions will have an effect on the breed, so it is important that you are sufficiently knowledgeable to make sensible decisions. While you cannot expect everyone to agree with your opinions, you must have in your own mind a very clear and reasonable justification for your placings. It does no-one any favours when people accept judging appointments before they are properly equipped for the job. Some, having campaigned a few Bulldogs for as many years, feel they are being left behind and embrace a judging career too soon. How often do we hear complaints that a certain person is up to judge when they been in the breed only five minutes. Fortunately, the criteria for a first-time championship judging appointment are under review.

Having discussed the perils of accepting a judging appointment too soon, it should also be said that older, more established judges who, after some time away, are called upon to provide a 'fresh approach', sometimes display the opinions of someone who is obviously out of touch and unacquainted with recent trends and developments within the breed.

Stewarding

Stewarding is an excellent way to familiarize yourself with ring procedure, and it is compulsory under proposed new rules for becoming a championship show judge. The requirements are to have stewarded for a minimum of three years and twelve shows at either open or championship level. The names and dates of these shows must be listed on the questionnaire that the aspiring championship show judge submits to the Kennel Club.

At shows in the United Kingdom, it is not uncommon for single dogs to be entered in several classes, and it is the steward's responsibility to place dogs in the order in which they were put in previous classes. Stewards will call the name of the class, and the numbers of the dogs entered. It is then the exhibitors' responsibility to ensure that they are at the ringside, ready for judging.

Try to be pleasant and helpful to all exhibitors without being too familiar; remember that many of them will be unacquainted with ring procedure and others will be nervous. Stewards normally check in on arrival with the show secretary, who will then issue them with a catalogue, rosettes and prize cards. As each dog enters the ring, the steward marks the dog's name in the catalogue, and makes a note of any absentees. Sometimes the steward will also be responsible for handing out numbered cards to each exhibitor; at other times these are already in place on the benches.

The Criteria for Judging

The important factor is that all judges should be experienced, competent and efficient. They should also be familiar with show regulations, ring procedure and the other practical aspects of showing and judging as well as having a thorough knowledge of the breed's anatomy, conformation, movement and, of course, the finer breed points.

Being a good judge is a hard thing to define. For instance, when reading a list of show results it may appear sometimes that a superior dog has been placed much lower than previously. However, it must be borne in mind that the judge can only assess the dogs as they appear on the day: the previously superior exhibit may well have been unwell or off colour, out of coat, or even perhaps lame on the day in question.

Breed Council Requirements

The Bulldog Breed Council require a minimum of seven years' judging experience within the breed (not just involvement within the breed) and to have judged a minimum of fifty classes to include at least three breed club open shows, with a minimum five-year period between the first and the last. One of these open shows must have been outside a one-hundred-mile radius of the candidate's residence.

Awarding Challenge Certificates

Judging books and marked catalogues should be kept and stored in a safe place as, one day – if you aspire to become a championship show judge of Bulldogs – you may be called upon to produce them. The Kennel Club criteria that the judge must meet in order to award CCs in the United Kingdom are currently under review, but the new proposals are as follows:

1. **Breeding/showing record**
The judge must have demonstrated successful showing experience and/or breeding programme. Save in exceptional circumstances, any first-time candidate is expected to have been owner/breeder of at least three dogs when they obtained their first entry in the Stud book.
2. **Requirements to write critiques**
The judge must state that he or she is prepared to write show critiques, as customarily submitted to the weekly dog press.
3. **Time before first CC appointment**
The judge must have a minimum of seven years' judging experience in the breed prior to awarding CCs for the first time.
4. **Requirements for previous stewarding experience**
The judge must have stewarded for a minimum of three years and twelve shows at either open or championship level.

For the judge's first CC appointment, Breed Council, national or parent or regional club assessor must send a confidential post-show report direct to the Kennel Club.

Note: assessors to be from list of up to fifteen people who have awarded the most CCs in the breed.

Judges' Lists

The judges' lists contain the names of all judges and their statuses. The Kennel Club will in future consider publishing the judges' own publication *The Kennel Gazette*, which will immediately make the judges' lists widely available and save considerable time and expense for breed clubs.

A1 List
Judges who have previously been approved to award CCs in a given breed and have carried out the appointment.

A2 List
Judges who, if invited to judge by a society, would in principle be approved by the Kennel Club to award CCs in a given breed for that occasion.

A3 List
Judges who are recommended by a bred council or breed club as being suitable to award CCs in the breed, but are not yet approved by The Kennel club for inclusion on an A2 list.

B List
Judges who have been approved by a breed council/club to judge at championship shows without CCs, or at open shows.

C Lists
Any C list drawn up by a breed council or breed club should comprise aspirant judges who do not fall into any of the above categories.

Your First Appointment

Start at the beginning, that is read everything you can lay your hands on, talk with experienced seniors in the breed, attend teach-ins and seminars and watch videos.

Aim for a few mixed classes: dogs and bitches that is. Usually half a dozen are on offer at the general open shows and these are a perfect way to embark on your judging career. Unfortunately many exhibitors give complimentary entries. These are no longer acceptable when you eventually fill in your application to the Kennel Club to award Challenge Certificates in Bulldogs. Many breed clubs hold Limit shows but the competition for judging at these is keen.

The first invitation will probably come via a phone call from a secretary who will enquire as to your availability to judge at any given time or place. This will be followed up by an official letter inviting you to judge; it may ask if you require any expenses for travel, fuel, accommodation, and so on. These are usually only offered for championship show appointments; you will normally be expected to judge open shows in an honorary capacity.

Once you have replied and accepted, the show secretary will then confirm your appointment, stating that this is now a binding agreement between you and the club or society. The Kennel Club take an extremely dim view of a judge who fails to turn up for an appointment and, unless there is a very sound excuse (such as a serious illness or perhaps an accident), the penalties imposed can be severe.

When making the initial offer, most clubs and societies will stipulate their conditions of your appointment, such as asking you not to judge the breed again within a given time and within a certain radius of their show, so consider carefully.

During the run-up to your appointment, avoid making comments about the breed or remarking on any particular dogs. When the day arrives you will probably have a totally different impression of the dogs on the day, and if you had in mind a dog that you were convinced would be your Best of Breed you will probably find he is not even entered. It is always wise to study the Breed Standard the night before to refresh your mind, especially on the finer points.

Be punctual, arriving in plenty of time to report to the secretary, collect your judging books, and to sit down for a coffee and some quiet reflection. Judging normally starts on the dot and, at general shows, Bulldogs are invariably first in the ring, which is common sense on the part of the society organizers when one considers the possible rise in temperature as the day wears on and the breed's susceptibility to heat.

Dress sensibly and appropriately. Women should remember that judging Bulldogs entails getting up and down countless times, so high heels and new shoes are to be avoided as you could be spending several hours on your feet. Men should, without exception, always wear

*Bulldog of the Year judge Bill Cartwright
(Brandywell Bulldogs) goes over
competitor Ch. Isgraig Bella Vega,
handled by her breeder Bill Roberts
(Photo: Simon Lathan.)*

shirt, tie and jacket. In hot weather it is perfectly acceptable to remove the jacket once judging has commenced, but never the tie. Short-sleeve shirts are fine; otherwise sleeves can be rolled up. Ties should be secured so as not to dangle over the exhibit. I once watched a judge wearing only a sleeveless quilted body warmer. Each time he stooped down to go over a Bulldog, his head completely disappeared inside like a tortoise. Many times I have stood by the ringside and watched overseas judges smoking or chewing gum and thought what a poor impression it relayed. Remember that while casual clothing may be acceptable for exhibitors, for a judge it conveys an air of indifference.

If you are second or maybe third in the ring, never wander too far away as exhibitors may be restless and eager to start as soon as the ring is available. Most will have other dogs at home, and many will have risen with the larks to travel, sometimes through the night, to reach the show.

Even though you may be familiar – even on first-name terms – with many of the exhibitors, it is generally considered bad form to address them personally. Avoid any possible contact with exhibitors before you commence judging as this could cause embarrassment. Once in the ring address all the exhibitors formally as Sir or Madam.

Perusing the Entry

The one question that I am always asked is 'How do I go over a Bulldog?' What follows is my preferred method; others will do things differently, but this is intended as a preliminary guide for the beginner.

In most coated breeds, careful and skilful grooming can cover a multitude of sins. But with the Bulldog it is mostly a case of what you see is what you get. An accomplished handler can conceal a poor topline or a weak front while the dog is in the line-up, but, with the best endeavours, all this will fall apart on the move.

Explain to the steward which direction you wish the line-up to face, bearing in mind that the ringside will want the best possible view. Let

Ch. Kelloe Maid in Silver. 'Peggy' was litter-sister to White Glove. Notice the beautiful turn, sweep and fit of her underjaw. (Photo: Pearce.)

the dogs enter the ring and give the handlers time to set them up. In many breeds it is customary for all the class entrants to go round the ring a few times. This is not the case in Bulldogs. They will begin to pant, spoiling their expression and making it difficult to close the mouth and check the bite when you later go over them.

Once they are all stacked up, I briefly walk along the front and then across the back of the line-up, usually pausing for a moment, behind each dog, when I look down to check the width of shoulders, rib, and pear-shaped body tapering down to the light hindquarters. Then call the first Bulldog into the front of the ring, facing the spectators. Give the handler sufficient time to stack the dog, then stand well back to see the outline, hind angulation, topline, and general overall balance.

Approach the dog head on, studying the front, looking for good bone, tight feet and pasterns, good depth of brisket, and tacked-on, not tight shoulders. Gently lift the flews to check dentition, paying attention to the width between the canines and checking to see that the underjaw is wide and not wry. Next check the width and depth of the foreface, looking to see that the width travels up to the nose and doesn't narrow into an 'A' shape. The nose should be black with wide nostrils. The top of the nose should be level with the eyes. Eyes should be dark, with little, if any, white showing when viewed head on. Check that the eyelids are well pigmented, a good fit and shape, not drooping or diamond-shaped. Also be aware of excessive moisture which could indicate entropion.

The skull should be well wrinkled, but not coarse or overdone, and ears should not fall forward like flaps (termed 'button' ears), nor should they be lively or stand on end (termed 'tulip' ears). Now place your hand under the dog's jaw and, supporting this, move round to the side. Look once again at the general symmetry of the head, paying attention to depth of foreface and layback. The dog should have reasonable reach and arch of neck and not appear stuffy. Check the topline, depth and width of chest and also tuck-up, paying attention to the length in loin and checking the tail-set.

Then rise and reach down over the dog, feeling the barrel of rib and making sure there is no gap or light between the shoulders and the rib. Looking down, one can observe if the dog is pear-shaped (something that will be missing if he is beefy behind), or too long in back. Then, with the males, check that he is entire, and run your hands down along the hindquarters to feel the angulation.

The best way to walk the Bulldog in the ring is in a triangle, and then finally straight up and down. Showmanship must be taken into consideration. If a dog moves spookily, jumping at any noise such as that made by a chair being blown over, or for some other reason moves erratically, allow both dog and handler to have another chance. Then either shake a bunch of keys or make a high-pitched noise to attract the dog's attention so that you can check the dog's expression and lively ears. Quite often, if the temperature is high and the dog is panting, he will momentarily close his mouth, allowing you to make a better assessment.

In large classes it is usually better to short list a selected few. However, if you are required to place, say, five dogs in the cards, try not to pull out six, embarrassing a lone loser. Always be positive and decisive, and above all polite. Judges who take an age to make up their minds are an irritation to exhibitors, who will find it difficult to keep dogs standing in show poses for any length of time.

Remember, no dog is perfect and they all have something about them that we would like to change.

Critiques

Although it is not necessarily obligatory to write, or as some put it, to furnish a critique, it will be expected as a common courtesy to the exhibitor. In these days of personal computers and word processors, or even just employing the help of a friend, it is not unreasonable to expect a few lines, however simple, on each dog. However, many just don't bother, hoping, mistakenly, that it will pass unnoticed.

To some, writing comes naturally; for the majority it can be a time-consuming and onerous chore. Some judges have a deep, qualified knowledge of the breed but, alas, are not particularly good showmen. They may feel somewhat uncomfortable and a little self-conscious at

The two CC winners at Crufts 1996 (left and opposite) *under the well-respected breed specialist, Mrs Ada Pitts. Ch. Medbull Gold Dust over Kelloe and ...*

being centre stage, and so they may enjoy doing their critiques to enlighten, further justify, and give an insight into their placings. Many a Bulldog can appear excellent front on although the fact that he may have a wry jaw or be totally lacking in rib will not be seen from the ringside, and a critique is a means of explaining this.

A balanced critique should take into account both faults and virtues, giving some indication of how the first, say, three in each class arrived in that order. I usually write some form of introduction giving my most recent observations and assessing whatever progress I may feel has been made since my last appointment, but also mentioning any particular points I may consider we are losing in the breed at that particular time.

There is a fine balance between being positive and over kind about all exhibits. Quite often, if a critique only mentions virtues there may be a tendency for exhibitors to assume that you may not have noticed a serious fault. One has to temper consideration with honesty but without labouring a point at the expense of spoiling a dog's show career. Hypercritical comments about dogs, especially about those who have over the current season been competing against the judge's own stock, reflect badly on the judge. Remarks such as 'Moved badly and his mouth is not his fortune', are not constructive and come across as being purely vindictive.

Critiques should be interesting and not repetitive, although it is difficult to avoid using the same terms when judging to type. Try to introduce some humour, encouraging exhibitors to read all the reports, not just their own, and avoid any large, unwieldy or ambiguous words. Try to avoid potted terms such as 'unlucky to meet first', as this is poor consolation to an exhibitor licking his wounds, and try not to generalize so much that it reads like a litany, i.e. 'nice front, nice body, good head, moved well'.

Critiques can be handwritten, using capitals for the dog's and owner's name and, if typed, always double-space the lines to assist the editor and typesetter. When completed, it can either be faxed direct or posted to the canine press in the stamped-addressed envelope that they normally supply to societies or clubs for this purpose.

Lastly, it always makes sense to write your critique while everything is still fresh in your mind's eye. It's not as bad as it seems and you will get great satisfaction when your finished work is out in print, so enjoy.

Once you have written a few critiques, you may get the taste for writing and feel inclined to submit other articles to the press. For five years I contributed to *Our Dogs* on a weekly basis as the Bulldog breed correspondent. Such a commitment can lose its novelty, though. Many are eager to write in order to get things off their chests; and yet – once this has been achieved and pride has been satisfied, when they are obliged to continue sending in notes every week – they find extreme difficulty in sustaining it.

When writing, consider the facts carefully and try to get to the point; avoid padding things out with small talk. When I first began to write, an established breed-note writer told, or rather warned, me that for some unknown reason, whatever you print, everyone thinks it is about them.

At the time of writing, 120 people are approved by the Kennel Club to judge at championship level (award CCs).

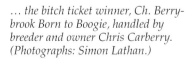

… the bitch ticket winner, Ch. Berrybrook Born to Boogie, handled by breeder and owner Chris Carberry. (Photographs: Simon Lathan.)

8

Breeding

Breeding Bulldogs is not something to embark on lightly. Success as a breeder takes many years of experience (with the accompanying heartbreaks and setbacks) coupled with an enquiring, intuitive and perceptive mind. Genetics, even at its simplest, is not a simple subject. However, dogs have been improving steadily generation by generation because breeders are increasingly better informed. Dogs mature rapidly and they reproduce themselves with great rapidity, advancing a generation in breeding each year. Not only do dogs reproduce themselves at an early age, but bitches ordinarily produce numerous puppies at each pregnancy, all of which enables the breeder to assess progress.

Responsibilities

The successful breeder of Bulldogs breeds not for the money but for the love of the breed. Naturally, the main aim is for the resulting puppies to be better specimens than the parent dogs. Unfortunately, many breeders, with the best intentions, lack a selective eye.

Before you contemplate breeding, you must consider whether you can reasonably commit yourself to the time and effort involved in rearing the puppies, such as feeding every two hours for the first two weeks. There is also the expense. The cost of a stud fee, time off work, the possibility of a costly Caesarean, veterinary fees resulting from complications, and the after care all adds up. You will also be responsible for attending to the bitch, and for placing the puppies in suitable, caring homes.

It will be your responsibility to breed stock as near to the Standard as possible. We are caretakers of this wonderful breed and, as such, are expected to pass on to future guardians better stock to breed on from than we inherited ourselves. Slow and sure is the name of the game when breeding Bulldogs: there are no short cuts for those wanting instant gratification.

Inherited Defects

The responsible breeder will take care to breed only from healthy stock. There are certain defects that are generally considered to replicate themselves, and dogs displaying these should not be bred from. These include most eye conditions, such as entropion, ectropion, dry eye, and prolapsed Harderian glands ('cherry eye'); respiratory complaints, such as pinched nostrils, soft palette, small, restricted or collapsed tracheas, heart murmurs; other defects such as ingrowing screw tails, hemivertebrae, slipping patellas and wry jaws; and, although not health-related, inferior attributes such as light eyes.

As breeders we must avoid bowing to fashion. If we can conserve the breed and perhaps improve the health aspect, we have done as much as can be expected.

In-Breeding and Line-Breeding

The terms line-breeding and in-breeding can be broadly defined as any duplication of dogs within a five-generation pedigree. The mating of cousins or Bulldogs sharing common grandparents is generally considered to be line-breeding; mating dogs of a closer relationship – brother to sister, father to daughter, mother to son – is usually considered to be in-breeding.

Like begets like. The only way to hold on to virtues with any degree of certainty is to breed from dogs of a fairly close relationship. They need to share the same genetic inheritance. Whatever fault your bitch has, the sire, and possibly his parents, must compensate on this point. Only study, expert advice and ultimately experience will help you follow these principles and avoid mistakes.

In-breeding can be a dangerous game in that as you double up on the good points, you may also compound the bad ones. However, some have inbred with marked success, and one could argue that you cannot make an omelette without breaking eggs, but it is not a method to be recommended to the inexperienced.

Outcrossing

Outcrossing is the mating of Bulldogs of completely different bloodlines with no, or only few, common ancestors. Outcrossing is used when undesirable traits begin to manifest themselves. The purpose is to introduce fresh, strong points to a line, but it can often introduce undesirable traits that were not evident before. These can sometimes take some time to breed out, and for this reason we always breed any resulting stock straight back into our own lines.

In the early 1990s I appeared to be on the right track with my breeding programme with good, well-balanced body shapes, correct conformation, and super movement. I was developing a distinct type, with strong bitches displaying the super turn and upsweep of underjaw inherited from Jacob. All that was lacking was width in underjaw, foreface, and a shade more overall bone.

I brought in a young white-ticked dog called Tugga Tough Decision for Kelloe. Boozer, as he was known to us, proved to be an admirable choice. He was a calculated risk in that he had very obvious faults – he was a little tight in shoulder, he lacked neck, and he was straight in topline – but I considered none of these points to be life threatening, and the gamble paid off. Ch. Kelloe White Glove was the fruit of one of these matings, and I always remember reading Norman Davis's (Ocobo) critique after he had judged the Northern Bulldog Championship Show and awarded her Best in Show. He commented that she had the largest underjaw of any Bulldog present today, dog or bitch!

The Brood Bitch

If you do not as yet own your own Bulldog bitch and are looking to start your own line, the best advice I can give is to phone around the breed clubs (*see* Useful Addresses) and enquire where and when they will be holding shows. At shows you can study the dogs being shown, also perhaps their progeny, and discuss your ideas with their breeders. Breed open shows are probably the best venues for this as breeders and exhibitors will be under less duress than at championship shows; the more relaxed, less formal surroundings will better enable you to mix with other Bulldog breeders and discuss your plans.

It is a commonly held view that the strength of a kennel lies in its bitches, although it does take two to tango! Once you have decided which lines you wish your foundation bitch to come from, contact the kennel owner. Bulldogs cannot be bred to order and it is highly unlikely that any puppies, especially bitches, will be available at that particular time. It is important to build and maintain some type of rapport with the breeder, as there could be a fairly lengthy wait for a litter.

This beautiful dog puppy has a superb width and depth of foreface. (Photo: Simon Lathan.)

Once you have acquired your brood-bitch, take an objective view of her and, no matter how much you love her, be brutally honest with yourself. Does she have a sound temperament and a well-balanced body shape, and does she fit the Standard? Does she exhibit any obvious faults or congenital defects? Always breed your best to the best because, as sure as night follows day, two inferior types will produce the same.

With breeding, the main thing is to be objective. It is pointless carrying on with something that is obviously not working, so be prepared to change direction and keep an open mind; be receptive to suggestions and new ideas. We are constantly, more often than not subconsciously, in the process of learning. Someone once commented to the artist Salvador Dali that they needed a change of direction, and his profound advice was to put their shoes on the opposite feet!

Lastly, you must consider the danger involved in any pregnancy. There is always a possibility that complications might arise and, in dire circumstances, be fatal to your beloved bitch. In saying this I am reminded of Minnie (Ch. Kelloe White Glove). Minnie loved to play and run for miles, but because there was always a show on the horizon, we had to restrict her, paranoid that an injury would occur. It is a big regret that I was unable to allow her the freedom to enjoy a more active, doggy life.

Soon after her retirement she came into season. I nervously decided to have her mated, something that I had always made excuses to put off as I sensed that once she had reared a litter she would never have gone back enough underneath to ever be shown again. I put her to my then newest young male, Ch. Kelloe Angel Dust: a superb pure-white powerhouse, dripping in bone and substance. I had carefully bred both parents and frankly this was to be the litter of the decade.

Fairly early on in the pregnancy I became increasingly alarmed at the rapid increase in her size. An ultrascan showed there to be at least ten puppies. By the time she had reached seven weeks she was very uncomfortable, carrying far too much fluid for my liking, and I was watching her day and night. Tragically she died in her bed in her sleep. I had never been so upset about anything, ever. I loved her dearly and it was the saddest day of my life.

Mating Minnie proved to be a mistake, and I would never again mate a bitch once she approached five years old. While I have always been of the mind that if no one had taken risks none of us would be here, it is also important to learn from your mistakes and avoid repeating them.

When to Mate Your Bitch

Bulldog bitches normally have their first season at about eight months of age and then approximately every six months thereafter. However, there are exceptions. I had one bitch, Champion Kelloe Maid in Silver, who approached thirteen months before her first season. There were many anxious visits to my vet who was preparing to administer medication to induce her season, but fortunately this course of action was not needed.

Generally it is possible to mate a Bulldog bitch on her second season, before she is two years old. I seldom mate bitches of more than four years old as older bitches are prone to complications, as we have seen. I have had some harrowing experiences. I have heard of those mating their bitches on their first season as the bitch is approaching one year old, justifying themselves by saying that in her natural habitat a bitch would be mated every season. However, our bitches are domestic dogs and not subject to the vagaries of natural selection in the way that their wild counterparts are. Even if they are physically mature I think it unfair to breed from such young bitches as they are still babies themselves and certainly not prepared for the trauma of motherhood.

It makes sense to discuss your plans for breeding a litter, well in advance, with someone experienced such as your bitch's breeder. Their

Ch. Broomwick Beatrix at Sutus, bred by John and Dorothy Jones and owned by Tony and Barbara Darmanin. (Photo: The Bulldog Club Inc.)

Gestation Table: Pregnancy and Whelping

Jan	Mar	Feb	Apr	Mar	May	Apr	Jun	May	July	Jun	Aug	July	Sep	Aug	Oct	Sep	Nov	Oct	Dec	Nov	Jan	Dec	Feb
1	5	1	5	1	3	1	3	1	3	1	3	1	2	1	3	1	3	1	3	1	3	1	2
2	6	2	6	2	4	2	4	2	4	2	4	2	3	2	4	2	4	2	4	2	4	2	3
3	7	3	7	3	5	3	5	3	5	3	5	3	4	3	5	3	5	3	5	3	5	3	4
4	8	4	8	4	6	4	6	4	6	4	6	4	5	4	6	4	6	4	6	4	6	4	5
5	9	5	9	5	7	5	7	5	7	5	7	5	6	5	7	5	7	5	7	5	7	5	6
6	10	6	10	6	8	6	8	6	8	6	8	6	7	6	8	6	8	6	8	6	8	6	7
7	11	7	11	7	9	7	9	7	9	7	9	7	8	7	9	7	9	7	9	7	9	7	8
8	12	8	12	8	10	8	10	8	10	8	10	8	9	8	10	8	10	8	10	8	10	8	9
9	13	9	13	9	11	9	11	9	11	9	11	9	10	9	11	9	11	9	11	9	11	9	10
10	14	10	14	10	12	10	12	10	12	10	12	10	11	10	12	10	12	10	12	10	12	10	11
11	15	11	15	11	13	11	13	11	13	11	13	11	12	11	13	11	13	11	13	11	13	11	12
12	16	12	16	12	14	12	14	12	14	12	14	12	13	12	14	12	14	12	14	12	14	12	13
13	17	13	17	13	15	13	15	13	15	13	15	13	14	13	15	13	15	13	15	13	15	13	14
14	18	14	18	14	16	14	16	14	16	14	16	14	15	14	16	14	16	14	16	14	16	14	15
15	19	15	19	15	17	15	17	15	17	15	17	15	16	15	17	15	17	15	17	15	17	15	16
16	20	16	20	16	18	16	18	16	18	16	18	16	17	16	18	16	18	16	18	16	18	16	17
17	21	17	21	17	19	17	19	17	19	17	19	17	18	17	19	17	19	17	19	17	19	17	18
18	22	18	22	18	20	18	20	18	20	18	20	18	19	18	20	18	20	18	20	18	20	18	19
19	23	19	23	19	21	19	21	19	21	19	21	19	20	19	21	19	21	19	21	19	21	19	20
20	24	20	24	20	22	20	22	20	22	20	22	20	21	20	22	20	22	20	22	20	22	20	21
21	25	21	25	21	23	21	23	21	23	21	23	21	22	21	23	21	23	21	23	21	23	21	22
22	26	22	26	22	24	22	24	22	24	22	24	22	23	22	24	22	24	22	24	22	24	22	23
23	27	23	27	23	25	23	25	23	25	23	25	23	24	23	25	23	25	23	25	23	25	23	24
24	28	24	28	24	26	24	26	24	26	24	26	24	25	24	26	24	26	24	26	24	26	24	25
25	29	25	29	25	27	25	27	25	27	25	27	25	26	25	27	25	27	25	27	25	27	25	26
26	30	26	30	26	28	26	28	26	28	26	28	26	27	26	28	26	28	26	28	26	28	26	27
27	31	27	May 1	27	29	27	29	27	29	27	29	27	28	27	29	27	29	27	29	27	29	27	28
28	Apr 1	28	May 2	28	30	28	30	28	30	28	30	28	29	28	30	28	29	28	30	28	30	28	Mar 1
29	Apr 2			29	31	29	July 1	29	31	29	31	29	30	29	31	29	Dec 1	29	31	29	31	29	Mar 2
30	Apr 3			30	June 1	30	July 2	30	Aug 1	30	Sep 1	30	Oct 1	30	Nov 1	30	Dec 2	30	Jan 1	30	Feb 1	30	Mar 3
31	Apr 4			31	June 2			31	Aug 2			31	Oct 2	31	Nov 2			31	Jan 2			31	Mar 4

First column lists mating date; second column lists whelping date.

help and advice may well be needed at some later date. Plan carefully, avoiding obvious pitfalls such as your bitch preparing to whelp the same day as your daughter's wedding or during the week on which you've booked your holiday. Check the gestation chart as these dates are tried and tested and pretty accurate.

How Many Puppies?

This is an interesting question. A small drop of a fertile dog's semen can contain millions of sperm – enough to fertilize every bitch in the country – but the number of puppies your bitch will produce is reliant on the number of eggs she releases for fertilization. To date, the largest successfully reared litter contained sixteen Bulldog puppies. My personal best was a litter of twelve, of which ten survived. I would consider five surviving Bulldog puppies to be an average, manageable-sized litter.

Choosing a Stud-Dog

Close line-breeding has been one of the main reasons for my stock's consistent winning at top-drawer level. I have never been particularly

One of the 1990s' prolific sires, Lynmans Living Legend, handled by breeder and owner Lyn Manns of Titchfield.

bothered as to whether my chosen stud-dog is a champion, although the red ink on a written pedigree does look impressive. In fact two of the breed's most prolific producers of champion stock during the 1990s were untitled, and so were their parents.

My own boy, Tugga Tough Decision for Kelloe, bred by Andrea Gautier Née Facey, sired six British champions including Ch. Kelloe White Glove (the breed record holder), and numerous overseas champions. Lynmans Living Legend, owned and bred by Lyn Manns has also sired six United Kingdom champions to date and was retired from showing whilst a youngster. In fact, I awarded him his only Challenge Certificate as a junior when I judged at Leicester Championship Show.

I am seldom bothered by what others may think, and instead I have taken chances which for the most part have paid off. In selecting a stud-dog I have paid little account to geographical location or personalities, i.e. the owners, but many do not have such a choice in these matters. One must select the dog, not the owner or the place the dog lives. Of course, you may have the ideal stud-dog living fairly close by, but you should never use a dog just because he lives down the road, nor dismiss out of hand a dog because of a personality clash with his owner.

There is a tendency for many breeders to use the flavour of the month, a particular dog that is doing well in the show ring. Time and time again I see breeders changing direction with their breeding programmes. Occasionally, on the law of averages, someone will hit lucky but their pedigrees are a bewildering mishmash of incompatible dogs. When setting out to lay the foundations for your own line, it is a mistake to start off with a plethora of bloodlines, although in this breed it is difficult to be too diverse as the gene pool is a small one, and most dogs are related to each other in the not too distant past.

Quite often, well-balanced top-winning dogs, although displaying few or little in the way of faults, may also display few virtues and therefore have little to contribute to a generally mediocre bitch, whereas an overdone, exaggerated dog with obvious faults may have corresponding virtues to pass on the bitch's progeny. Many times I have seen matings between top-winning champion dogs and champion bitches result in litters of unremarkable puppies. Each animal had an exemplary pedigree but they were not particularly compatible. Many consider their bitch's faults and then choose a stud-dog with corresponding virtues hoping to do a balancing act, only to find that in a litter of, say, four, two take after the mother and two the sire.

I always suggest that the newcomer goes along to shows with classes for the breed on offer, better still a club open or championship show.

Look at the dogs that appeal to you and consider why; look to see if their progeny are winning in the ring and, most importantly, whether they are the type you are aiming to produce. Most important, does he say to you, Bulldog? If possible, approach the owners of the stud-dog. They will probably have many years' experience and a wealth of knowledge to offer, and they will probably give you an honest assessment of your bitch.

On a lighter note, I remember a frustrated champion-bitch owner bitterly complaining that she had been mated to virtually every prolific sire in the country with no result. For months there was silence and then the news broke: his bitch was pregnant, but to his Whippet! Whilst on the subject I recall seeing a second-generation Bulldog-Newfoundland while judging in Germany. The dog, who had come from Denmark, was very attractive, looked typically like a Bulldog except that he had long curly hair, resembling a giant Abyssinian guinea pig.

Oestrus

Most Bulldog bitches have their first season at eight months of age and then at six-monthly intervals. When your bitch is nearing oestrus you will be expected to contact the owner of the stud-dog and book his dog's services. At the same time you will need to agree terms such as stud fees, picks of litter, and arrangements for repeat matings should your bitch miss. As soon as the season starts you will need to inform the stud-dog owner so that he can ensure he is available and has not booked the same dog to another bitch.

On the assumption that your bitch is of the correct age, that she has been transferred into your name, that you have chosen and arranged to mate her to the dog of your choice, you must watch for the following signs. A slight swelling and pinkishness of the vulva,

Ch. Merriveen Pepsi Cola, owned and bred by Pat Dellar. (Photo: Pearce.)

accompanied by a light-coloured blood known as 'colour'. As the season progresses the blood will become brighter and the flow will increase. The vulva will also swell quite dramatically in size until around the tenth or eleventh day, when the colour will begin to subside. This is normally a good indication that your bitch is ready for mating. If when you try tickling her vulva, she lifts her tail and adopts a mating stance, you can take this as a good indication that the time for mating is imminent.

As with all things in Bulldogs, there are no hard and fast rules here. Often a slight swelling and a tiny show of colour will be the only indication; these are termed 'silent seasons'. Here you must watch her closely, checking her vulva a few times each day with white tissue. On these occasions we have mated bitches five days after the onset of oestrus and had successful litters. If the bitch looks large enough and supple enough to accept a dog it can often be worth a try.

Most breeders like to have at least two matings, on the eleventh and thirteenth days. The sperm stays alive for several days so this method ensures that you cover most of the time that the bitch will be ovulating. Vets can also carry out fairly accurate blood test and vaginal smears to predict the best times for mating.

Mating

It is the generally accepted practice that the bitch always goes to the dog. But before the mating – and ideally before oestrus – you should take your bitch to the vet for a general health check-up and worming (*see* Chapter 10).

Over the years I have 'started off' dozens of different Bulldog males on their stud careers and every one has been different. Many have been quiet, sensitive types that have had to be patiently coaxed, the whole gruelling process taking hours of back-breaking work on cold floors. Others have been virtual rapists and the whole procedure has been over in minutes. Some dogs have been over-excitable and have required a firm tone and an even firmer hand; others have been gentle souls, and with the slightest raising of the voice all would have been lost.

There was one occasion on which I have regretted not having a video camera to hand. The dog was Sandcraft Baloo of Kelloe, who won one CC here before going over to Spain where he won the World Championship title in 1992. The late Harold Hayball had brought a rather nice bitch to be mated, and we were all set, the bitch in place over his knee.

Ch. Portfield So Small, owned and bred by Sheila Goddard. (Photo: Pearce.)

The dog entered the room, walked up to the bitch, sniffed her rear end and then casually trotted round to look at her face. The next thing we knew he had bolted to the other end of the room, straight into his travelling box, where he spun round, lifted his paw, and slammed the door behind him.

Many old timers in the breed use the tried and tested mating bench upon which the bitch rests. This is a horseshoe-shaped stirrup on adjustable metal stands, although I consider it to be a somewhat medieval implement. I prefer the adjustable, plastic, oblong boxes, used these days for step aerobics. They don't slip, are easily adjusted, and even easier to keep clean.

Things must always be as controlled as possible. I dislike the practice of letting the dogs play around, getting to know each other. An unnerved bitch can easily act out of character and turn on the dog and they can both end up exhausted and panting.

Bulldog matings are best performed with three helpers: one, preferably the bitch's owner, to hold her firmly with a leather collar, and if she struggles a little to pull down (a leather collar will not impede her breathing); a second person to sit on a cushion and place his leg over the plastic bench, with his foot against a wall or hard surface, and to lay the bitch's hind quarters over his leg; the third person to introduce and control the dog, to encourage the dog to mount the bitch, and to guide the dog's penis into the vagina by placing his fingers either side of the vulva.

As the dog thrusts, the penis will go into the vagina and then up and over. Here I tend to lift the dog's rear end slightly to help him up and over into the bitch. It helps also if the person with the bitch over his knees pulls the bitch's rear feet together and holds them securely. No two bitches are the same: some do the bucking bronco bit, while others stand as good as gold.

The Tie

Most dogs 'tie' during mating, that is the bulb at the base of the penis swells within the vagina and is clasped by the vaginal muscles, effectively locking the mating pair together. While the tie is not essential to conception, I always feel that a tied mating is the most reliable type: most of our bitches that have tied during mating have conceived. Bulldogs can stay tied for up to forty-five minutes, so it is essential that any mating during the summer months is carried out in the cool of the evening; you should also ensure that there is plenty of cool, fresh water to hand, and good ventilation in the room.

At some point during the tie, the dog will usually turn himself around so that bitch and dog stand tail to tail. It is generally believed that this is because, in the wild, opposite-facing partners are better able to ward off intruders from any direction. It also allows the bitch some relief from the weight of the dog on her back. However, most Bulldogs will be unable to turn themselves without assistance. You will need to stand over the dog and place your right arm under the dog's chest while your left hand holds the left leg. Then lift the dog's chest over to the right side of the bitch while at the same time lifting his left rear leg to clear the bitch's back. You should finish with the dog and bitch facing in opposite directions.

One could be forgiven for thinking this was a porcelain statue. (Photo: Simon Lathan.)

Both partners may go straight off to sleep; other times you may find that the dog becomes restless and wants to dismount. Care should be taken to prevent this before the dogs have released each other; either partner trying to pull away can damage the other.

Artificial Insemination

I have mixed feelings on this subject, as with the use of elective Caesars (*see* Chapter 9). If we have the know-how and technology, why not use it? After all, one could argue that the calculated and controlled 'natural' mating of a bitch is little more than rape. Many bitches parade themselves wantonly in front of males when they are approaching the correct time of their cycle to be mated, lifting their vulva towards the dog, but to many, especially a maiden bitch, the whole procedure is a frightening experience and artificial insemination might be a less traumatic method. Under Kennel Club rules in the UK, artificial insemination is permitted only in exceptional circumstances, and KC approval must be obtained well in advance of a proposed mating. In the breeding of cattle, in fact most livestock both here and overseas, the procedure is commonplace and has been in use for many years.

I have assisted a leading Bulldog breeder in Sweden, using artificial insemination (AI). The bitch was comfortable and relaxed, totally unaware that insemination had taken place. On the down side, breeding by AI does not carry the success rate of a natural mating. The temperature has to be exactly correct, and the procedure can lead to an infection in the bitch and discomfort for the dog.

Many find the frozen-semen concept exciting. The sperm is deep frozen in straws or phials, which means that famous or prolific dogs of yesteryear can continue to sire litters many years after their demise. I for one am not convinced that there is anything positive to be gained from using frozen semen. If anything it means going back on ourselves, and I see little value in that unless the breed developed, say, a congenital fault in future litters, when reversion to earlier stock might be useful. In any case, ideas change, fashions in Bulldogs change, and I wonder how true our memories are when we exalt the dogs of past decades.

Sending a Puppy Overseas

The UK has long been held in high esteem as the home of the Bulldog, and we are considered to have among the finest livestock and bloodlines in the world. For this reason, as you become an established and respected breeder, you may be contacted by overseas breeders, looking to improve and complement their existing stock.

Dogs for export must be over ten weeks of age to be accepted by most airline carriers, and after twelve weeks of age some importing countries will require vaccination against rabies. Many countries now stipulate that dogs are either tattooed or micro-chipped for identification purposes, and an Export Health Certificate, filled in, signed and stamped by an LVO (Licensed Veterinary Officer) can be obtained by contacting your local office of the Ministry of Agriculture, Fisheries and Food.

Make sure you satisfy yourself that the weather is temperate at the particular time of the year that you wish to send the puppy. Some countries, especially in southern Europe or the far East, have blistering temperatures during the months of June, July and August. Dogs have been known to be left unattended in boxes on airport tarmac runways while staff change over; and with temperatures soaring into the hundreds, tragedy is the result.

You will also need to contact the Kennel Club and apply for an Export Pedigree so that the new owner, if the dog has been sold, will be able to register the new arrival in his new country for showing and breeding purposes.

Affixes and Prefixes

An affix or prefix is the 'trademark' by which a kennel is known. Kelloe is the name of our kennel and, as with all affixes, it is registered at the Kennel Club. Nobody else can use this name, and it is added to all the names of all the dogs we own or breed. Each year we pay a small fee to retain the right to use the affix.

An affix can be obtained only by contacting the Kennel Club, who issue a form. On this you will be asked to give a choice of preferred names and these are, in due course, published in *The Kennel Gazette*. If there are no objections lodged against your choice of affix – such as too closely resembling another affix or even being the same as one already in use – the Kennel Club will inform you of the committee's decision.

It is common practice to place your affix in front of the name of a dog you have bred; it is then sometimes termed a prefix. If the dog was bred by someone else, you will be expected to add your kennel name to the end of the name, and it is termed an affix.

9

Pregnancy and Whelping

Once your bitch has been successfully mated, there is little need to change any of her routine, apart from taking care not to let her near other dogs until you are certain that her season has completely finished. A bitch can easily conceive to more than one dog over the period that she is ovulating, which, apart from possibly resulting in undesirable progeny, will confuse the date for whelping.

Signs of Pregnancy

You may detect slight changes in your bitch's behaviour, such as her becoming quieter and more affectionate. Many consider a creamy discharge from the vagina a few weeks after mating as a good sign and, after three to four weeks, look for enlargement and pinkishness of the teats.

At five weeks, a litter will begin to show as the bitch thickens along the flanks, and you can now begin steadily to increase her food intake. It is a common mistake to suppose that your bitch will require more food prior to this time (*see* Antenatal Care, opposite).

Ultrasonic Scanning

Sophisticated equipment such as the ultra-scan is now able to diagnose pregnancy. The correct time for its use is around four weeks into your bitch's pregnancy. In my experience, if the vet is able to tell you that four puppies can be seen on the scanning monitor, the chances are that she will have seven or eight. Even so, an estimate of the number of puppies (whelps) can prove useful if complications arise later. The procedure is quick, simple and easy. The bitch is carefully turned upside down or laid on her side. The veterinary nurse will sometimes prefer to shave away some of the underside hair. A gel-like substance is liberally applied and then an electronic probe is gently moved up and down the underside. It is usually fairly easy to see any puppies, and I have known times when I have been able to see their eyes. The main drawback of scanning is the initial expense of the equipment. If your vet does not have one, I am sure that they will know of somebody, perhaps a mobile unit, within your area.

False Pregnancy

This condition is quite common in Bulldog bitches, and it makes the detection of actual puppies extremely difficult. Here the use of simple blood test or ultrasonic scanning equipment comes in so useful.

Bitches may sometimes go the entire length of their time displaying all the symptoms of a real pregnancy, including the production of copious quantities of milk. Your vet will be able to help with medication to dry up the unwanted milk, but it is advisable to keep an eye on the bitch's teats, as these can become inflamed and hardened, which in extreme cases could result in the necessity for a mastectomy. Constant vigilance and regular massage can be of great help in keeping them soft and supple.

Antenatal Care

During the first twenty-one days of pregnancy, there is little necessity to add to her regular diet. However, if you feel the need to give some form of supplement, cottage cheese made from soured milk is a good and useful source of protein, calcium and phosphorus, but avoid commercial supplements as these often contain the mineral calcium.

When your bitch is in the later stages (over five weeks), increase her protein intake with cottage cheese and meat such as liver or heart, and eggs, making sure that the whites are thoroughly cooked. High-calorie foods should be decreased, and mineral and vitamin supplements such as cod-liver oil can be added at this point. At this stage, some breeders like to start giving raspberry leaf, a herbal supplement that is renowned for easing whelping.

Consult and keep in touch with your vet and, as your bitch grows, start to give several small meals a day. The pressure of the growing embryos on the abdominal organs may cause the bitch to be reluctant to take any large or bulky meals.

Worming

Nobody knows your own bitch better than you, so try to work out when she is due in season and administer a wormer before mating. If this has been overlooked, ask your vet for advice on a wormer that is safe to give once your Bulldog is in whelp.

Exercise

Initially, continue as before. As the pregnancy progresses, your bitch will start to slow down of her own accord. It is of the utmost importance that she should not become corpulent or soft but be kept firm and hard by giving the the optimum amount of exercise. A fat, floppy bitch is much more likely to experience whelping problems, and excess weight puts undue strain on the heart and joints. The bitch must not be allowed under any circumstances to run up or down stairs or jump to or from heights, climb on and off furniture unaided, or indulge in any form of strenuous games with other dogs.

Preparation for Whelping

Whelping Quarters

Decide which area of your home is to be designated the whelping area. It should be somewhere quiet, warm and secure, with access to a garden or exercise area for the bitch to clean herself. Introduce your bitch to her new living quarters at least two weeks before her confinement, and aim to keep the whelping-room temperature at a constant 75°F (24°C).

You will need a whelping box large enough for the bitch to lie outstretched in every direction. It should be fitted with a hinged front and a 'pig rail' around the inside, about 4in (10cm) away from the floor and from the sides. The low, hinged front will allow the bitch access in and out, while at the same time preventing the puppies from following her out. The pig rail safeguards the puppies from a clumsy bitch's accidentally crushing them against the box sides. The box should be set up off the floor, and totally draught-proof.

In times of yore, whelping boxes were of the wooden, usually home-made variety, which were easily chewed by both bitch and puppies alike. They were very difficult to clean, and very unhygienic. Nowadays there are several companies manufacturing all shapes and sizes of strong, sterile, fibreglass or polypropylene whelping box. Whichever type you choose, make sure that the floor surface is an easily washable type, as the bitch will no doubt have a few accidents, and in any event will possibly continue to pass blood clots and other matter for up to a week after whelping.

The box should be lined with layers of newspapers and thick, green-backed lambswool or 'Vetbed'-type fleecy bedding. This can be obtained from your local pet shop, trade stands at dog shows, or by post from suppliers listed in the weekly canine press. It is at this stage that you should ask all your friends to start religiously collecting all manner of newspaper as bale loads will be needed over the whelping and rearing period.

Equipment

You will need a heated lamp suspended over the whelping box. Some breeders like the infra-red bulbs, but I always feel that while they provide good heat they also give an extremely bright unnatural light and the bitch never seems to get the peace and quiet she craves. For this reason, I prefer the dull emitter type bulbs. These lamps should be suspended overhead by a chain attached to either a secure stand or a wall bracket, such as those employed for hanging baskets. Make sure that the lamp is high enough not to come into contact with the bitch's head and that it is extremely secure.

Heated Pads

These are small heated pads or electric blankets, obtainable form either high street chemists or home-brewing outlets. They are normally coated with plastic for safety purposes and have a thermostat temperature control with three settings. The pad should be wrapped in a pillowcase and then placed in a cardboard box that is large enough to allow the pups to edge their way off the pad if they become too warm. This box is an ideal incubator in which to place newborn pups while you return to assist the bitch, or for placing puppies born by Caesarean section. Heat can kill puppies as easily as cold draughts, so keep the heated pad on its lowest setting and prevent draughts by lightly covering the box with a tea-towel.

Some breeders acquire the clear plastic enclosed incubators, which maintain a constant temperature and are completely draught-free, but personally I dislike these as I believe them to be a breeding ground for bacteria.

Hot-Water Bottles
You will need a good old-fashioned hot-water bottle, half-filled with heated water, wrapped in towelling, and placed in another cardboard box, just in case there is a complication and a Caesarean section has to be performed by your vet. The puppies will be placed in this box for the journey home, and the box lightly covered by a tea-towel to exclude any draughts.

Checklist of Items for the Whelping Room

1. A note-pad bearing the phone numbers of your vet and any experienced Bulldog friends. You will need a reliable pen to register the time of the first strains and the time of each birth, along with the whelp's sex, colour and weight, and to record whether or not each afterbirth has presented itself.
2. A screw-top or sealable plastic-topped jar filled with sterilizing fluid of the sort used for baby utensils. Place inside some blunt-ended scissors and ready-cut lengths of cotton thread to tie the umbilical cord.
3. Permanganate of potash for sealing umbilical cords, cotton-wool buds and cotton-wool balls.
4. A large supply of good-quality, perforated kitchen-towel rolls.
5. Kitchen scales to weigh the puppies as soon as they are born.
6. A Lasix or similar electrolyte solution dissolved in a good-sized bowl of fresh water. Your bitch will need to sustain herself. Honey or glucose are good substitutes for Lasix.
7. A black plastic bin liner of the stronger variety, to place all the newspaper and wrapped afterbirths.
8. Clean, preferably white, thin-cotton gloves. These are excellent for gripping slippery puppies and their placentas.
9. Some brandy or, as I prefer, Dopram (supplied by the vet), which is invaluable for helping to 'kick start' a seemingly lifeless puppy.
10. An easy chair for yourself.
11. A cushion or comfortable pad to kneel on.
12. A television.
13. A tape, radio or CD player to give background music and help soothe the bitch.
14. Access to tea- and coffee-making facilities, and of course a good book, such as this one!

A contented Mum with her offspring. I don't think the newspaper headlines express her sentiments!

First-Stage Labour

Many Bulldog bitches carry their puppies on their sides like pannier bags. This can look awful and the bones sticking up out of the spine make your poor girl look a pathetic sight, like an old, broken-down mule. But you will be pleasantly surprised to see just how quickly the bitch will rally after whelping.

The first stage of labour will bring with it a distinct change in your bitch's behaviour. She will probably start to refuse food, and she may begin vomiting. However, I have known some bitches to eat heartily right up to giving birth, although it is unwise to allow access to food because if there are complications at a later stage some form of anaesthetic may be required. Restrict food but if your bitch requires water, give little and often.

Other signs will be the scratching or tearing up of paper and generally trying to nest. She may start spinning round in circles, or make short sharp barks for no apparent reason. Shivering or panting will both intensify, and her temperature will start falling from 101.5°F (38.6°C) down to about 98°F (36.5°C). (For guidance on taking your bitch's temperature, *see* Chapter 10.) As the temperature begins to rise, the next stage of whelping is now imminent and it is advisable to inform your vet. By now her vulva will have become enlarged, loose and floppy and you may notice a clear mucous discharge.

Second-Stage Labour

The next stage is when the bitch quietens down and starts to strain, almost as if she were trying to defecate. You will notice a far-away, staring look in her eyes and, as she strains, a rippling along her flanks. There will be a fair amount of discharge, the colour varying from clear to dark greenish-brown. The bitch may try to lick this up, and there is no reason why she should be prevented from doing so.

Within the first hour of straining, the first whelp, inside its fluid-filled bag, should present itself from the vulva. The puppy may be in an anterior position (head first), or posterior (feet first) in which case you may have to help ease the puppy out. Thin cotton gloves are a great help here as your own hands will quickly become slippery. The breed is famous for breach births in which either the rump or only one leg is presented. You may well experience this. Gently push a scrubbed-clean finger a small way into the vagina and carefully try to ease out the other leg, which may possibly have become stuck. Once you have both legs held gently, wait for the next contraction, at which point you should firmly tug the puppy, making sure that you pull the whelp down and slightly underneath the bitch. It is essential to pull only at the same time as the next contraction. If you have not been able to remove the whole puppy during this contraction, you must wait until the next contraction to try again. Every effort should be made to remove the puppy the first time, though, as time is of the essence at this stage. Any delay can result in the puppy's sac breaking or the umbilical cord rupturing, causing suffocation.

Once the first puppy has been born, the next should present itself within the hour. If nothing appears to be happening as time approaches two hours, speak with your vet.

As each puppy is born, carefully remove it from the mother, making a fuss and reassuring her constantly. Immediately break away the water sac or membrane from around the pup's head. Check the mouth for any obstructions. Then carefully hold the puppy with both hands and, with its head secured, swing the puppy up and down to dislodge any fluid or mucous from its mouth and lungs. Rub the puppy quite vigorously to improve the circulation and clear the airway. Often, an apparently limp, lifeless puppy will suddenly gasp as its lungs become

Contented puppies suckling. (Photo: Simon Lathan.)

clear, but this can sometimes take several minutes. Look for a strong active pup with good breathing and a good pink colour. If there is no response after a good few minutes' working on the puppy, try a drop of Dopram or, if unavailable, brandy on the tongue.

Cutting the Cord

Using the prepared sterilized cotton thread, tightly tie the umbilical cord at about 1in (2.5cm) from the pup's tummy. This seals the blood flow; you can now use the sterilized scissors to cut away the afterbirth. You will be surprised at how tough the cord is to cut. Experienced breeders will pinch the cords together and tear them apart with their fingers: something you can try at some later stage when you have more expertise. Some mothers have been known to break the cord with their teeth and then eat the placentas. This is quite harmless; in fact the afterbirths contain important nutrients for the bitch. However, excessive consumption can have a laxative effect, so you may want to limit the number she eats. The remaining cords will quickly dry up and usually drop off within the next few days. If the cord has been torn off or is bleeding profusely, something that happens when the puppy is presented without its sac, apply a little permanganate of potash with a cotton-wool bud.

Always take great care with umbilical cords as any straining can led to unsightly hernias requiring surgical treatment at a later date. The 'belly button' as we term it, is the easiest way for infections to enter the puppy's system, so it must be kept scrupulously clean and safe from any exposure to infection.

The New Puppy

Introduce the pup to its mother, making a fuss and encouraging her to let it feed. Sucking on the bitch's teats will help induce the next whelp and stimulate the flow of milk. The vital first feed is essential to get the colostrum, containing the mother's antibodies, into the vulnerable pup. While the pup is feeding, remove any afterbirth and make a note of it. Sometimes a placenta will be retained but then present itself during the next strains when you can carefully ease it away, using kitchen towel and taking care not to pull too tightly. If it is still securely attached, pulling can lead to excessive bleeding.

Newborn pups must be weighed and identified and logged, for example Bitch, white/red ear etc. Don't be too disconcerted by the variations in weight as these will often level out as the pups begin regular feeding.

Hold the pup in front of the bitch and encourage her to lick and clean the lower regions. This stimulates the puppy to empty its bowels and bladder, which is most important as its system will contain toxins that need to be flushed out. If the mother is unable or unwilling to do this, use cotton wool soaked in warm water solution with an added drop of washing-up liquid to simulate the bitch's licking. Gentle rubbing will make the puppy urinate, usually a bright-orange urine and sometimes at first a browny colour. Pay attention to the tail area: the puppy will probably not defecate every time but if it has a close or tight-fitting tail the anus may become either sore or tightly clogged, which will stop the puppy from passing his motions.

Caesareans

Certain problems may sometimes necessitate a Caesarean section. Inertia, large water babies or hydrocephalus pups (*see* Complications, page 161) are examples. It is fairly uncommon, but pelvic abnormalities can also prevent the bitch from passing the puppies as well as fibrous bands or maybe tumours, although you could possibly have noticed these when mating the bitch.

If, for whatever reason, a Caesarean is necessary, I prefer my bitches, who are show bitches, to have what is termed a mid-line cut. This is where the bitch is operated on while lying on her back and the pups are removed from the centre cut. The hair in this area is sparse and easy to clip away, there is very little visible scarring, and the wound nestles safely between the mammary glands and away from the sharp claws of the feeding puppies while it heals. Make sure your vet is familiar with this method and uses the firmer stitching techniques to compensate for the extra stress in this area. Your vet will advise as to when the

A ten-day-old puppy, ready to start opening his eyes. (Photo: Simon Lathan.)

stitches need to be removed (usually in about ten days). Some vets pre-fer to go in from the side or flank, but there is a lot of muscle in this area, which must be passed to gain access to the womb, and the result-ing scars look rather unsightly.

Your vet will normally tube your bitch and then work quickly to remove the pups before they are affected by the anaesthetic. This means the more hands the better. You will need to have ready your box with a hot-water bottle wrapped in towels for the journey home. As soon as each whelp is removed from its sac it should be rubbed briskly, once again, holding the head and shoulders firmly together in line with the body and swinging the pup downwards to remove any fluid from the lungs and throat (*see* page 154).

Elective Caesar

Strictly, a Caesarean section is a life-saving procedure that is carried out as a last resort, when there is no other practical method of deliver-ing the puppies. However, nowadays Caesarean sections tend to be routinely used on Bulldogs to avoid having to perform them on an emergency basis. In such cases, breeders book their bitches on the sixty-first day. This is termed an elective Caesar.

This approach can cause problems in itself, as most bitches are mated on more than one occasion during their season. The breeder has to be quite sure of exactly which mating the bitch conceived, other-wise the placentas will tear away from the uterus and could cause excessive bleeding.

157

Postpartum Care

Care of the Bitch

Keep a close eye on your bitch, especially if she has had a Caesarean. You will probably be shocked at how emaciated, sorrowful and pathetic she looks as she comes round from the anaesthetic. Once the first few days are past and she is back home in familiar surroundings you will be relieved at just how quickly she begins to pull round. I have known bitches to return home after surgery and head straight for the food dishes! Keep a close eye on her wound, making sure it is clean and free from infection. Your vet will advise as to when he wants to remove the stitches, normally after ten days. She will continue to discharge a mixture of brown clotted blood and bits of placenta, probably for the next few weeks.

After whelping, your bitch will be very thirsty and need plenty of fresh water. Make sure that she doesn't drink too much at any one time as this could well make her vomit. Keep a close eye on her teats. These can easily become sore or inflamed and gentle massage will prevent them from going hard, a sign of the onset of mastitis (*see* Complications, page 161).

Hygiene

After living through the years of parvovirus scares I am particularly careful each time I handle the pups, washing my hands in a solution and spraying my shoes each time I enter the puppy room. Naturally, friends and relations will be curious and eager to see the new puppies but this should be restricted, for the first few weeks at least. Peace, quiet and a draught-free room with a constant temperature of between 75 and 80°F (24 and 26.5°C) is absolutely essential.

Feeding

For the first two weeks the puppies must be put on to the bitch for feeding every two hours, day and night. Here you must be completely disciplined; your life must revolve around this regime. After each feeding session the pups must be put safely back into their box, on the heated blanket, and this covered with a tea towel. Take great care to place this box fairly high up and away in a safe place. I have heard tales of Bulldog mothers managing to scale kitchen worktops or open doors, and then to be found asleep on top of the box and all the puppies suffocated.

158

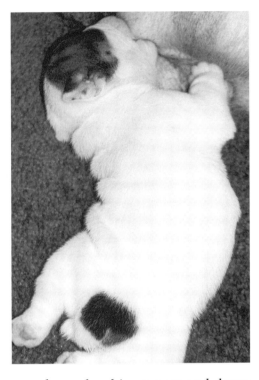

A puppy will slip off the bitch's nipple when it has finished suckling. A nice fat tummy is a good indication that the puppy is feeding well. (Photo: Simon Lathan.)

Naturally if you give constant supervision, puppies can be left with a loving mother for countless hours. On the other hand you cannot afford to oversleep or pop out for an extended shopping trip. Puppies can dehydrate at an alarming rate and it is of vital importance to keep their systems flushed at all times.

Watch carefully as the puppies suckle, and try to move them around on the different teats. Some teats produce a lot more milk than others. Also, there will always be one hyperactive puppy who makes his way up and down the line, pushing all the others off their teats. Once the puppies have finished feeding and seem contented, or sometimes between feeds, I will give them a milk supplement. I administer this in a banana-shaped bottle with a rubber teat. This shape bottle is particularly good as it can be rocked back during the feeding if the puppy appears to be taking in too much milk at any point. Excess ingestion of milk is indicated when milk begins to bubble around the puppy's nose. Make sure you sterilize the bottle and teat before feeding each puppy separately, as each pup has his own 'personalized' *E. coli* so it is best to avoid cross-infections.

After the first couple of weeks you will find that you can start stretching the night feeds from two to three, and eventually to four hours. It is surprising how quickly you acclimatize to nocturnal living; I have been doing it for years!

Tube Feeding
This is an invaluable, fast and effective way to get nutrients and fluids into a weak or dehydrated puppy. As with everything in life, it is easy when

At ten days the eyes are gradually starting to open. Check the nails, and nip off just the very tips. (Photo: Simon Lathan.)

you know how, but demonstration is necessary. Approach either your vet or an experienced breeder who will show you how to do it safely.

Worming Puppies

Consult your vet for advice on which particular wormer to use. The preparations are available in drops or paste form, either of which is usually administered after the first week. Worming will have to be repeated. Your vet will tell you how often to worm.

Nails

Puppies' nails can be extremely sharp on the sensitive skin around the mother's milk-gland area. As they also grow like weeds, nip off just the very tips on a regular basis. Nails are also a good gauge as to the puppies' general health: any excessive whitening or bright-white spotting usually points to a calcium deficiency.

160

Complications in the Bitch

Eclampsia

This is fairly common and is caused by low circulating blood calcium. It is easily remedied with an intravenous injection of soluble calcium, which must be administered by a vet, or by giving liquid calcium directly into the back of the mouth with an oral syringe. It occurs most frequently just before the bitch whelps or at around three weeks after whelping when her milk resources are under their heaviest demand.

Though the cure is straightforward, the condition is extremely serious, so if you suspect your bitch may have eclampsia, call your vet without delay. The signs are varied from panting and unsteadiness on her feet to uncontrollable shaking of the head from side to side. There is a high temperature and constant dripping of saliva.

Inertia

There are two types of inertia: primary and secondary.

A bitch in primary inertia does not progress beyond the first stage of labour. She will have shown all the preliminary signs of whelping, but then fails to produce any effective contractions. Susceptibility to inertia may be hereditary, but it can also occur in a bitch that is ill at ease for any reason. An injection administered by the vet may solve the problem; otherwise, a Caesarean is necessary.

Secondary inertia occurs during the second stage of labour. Contractions will have started and the bitch may even have produced puppies, but then the contractions cease. The cause is likely to be either exhaustion or an obstruction in the birth canal. A short rest may be all that is needed, but if the bitch's contractions fail to resume within two hours of delivering the last puppy then veterinary assistance is necessary. Depending on the cause, the vet will either administer an injection or perform a Caesarean.

When one of my bitches experienced inertia, the vet performed a Caesarean section to find a litter of twelve – the largest litter I have bred. The bitch had only ten teats for her twelve offspring.

Post-Whelping Metritis

This is a serious condition which may arise as a result of a retained placenta or a difficult labour. It occurs within about twenty-four hours of whelping and is characterized by a high temperature and a brown, foul-smelling discharge. A greenish-brown discharge is normal after whelping; but if you are in doubt about the condition of your bitch, consult your vet.

Mastitis

This is an inflammation of the milk glands and while it is usually seen in bitches that are feeding pups it can also be occur in maiden bitches and those in false pregnancy (*see* page 149).

The symptoms are redness and painful swelling of the teats, and the bitch may even go off her food or run a temperature. Consult your vet.

Complications – the Puppies

Cleft Palate

As soon as each pup is moving vigorously and ready to be put aside for the next one, tilt back the head, open the mouth and check the roof for signs of a cleft palate. This appears as a slit or serrated groove and will make it difficult for the puppy to suckle. Feed will eventually bubble up through the nose, the rest making its way down into the lungs, resulting in death through pneumonia. For this reason it is always best to have the puppy put down.

Many years ago we kept a cleft-palated puppy alive for months, by careful hand rearing and tubing until he was considered old enough by the vet to carry out corrective surgery. He lived for many years with friends as a family pet, although he stayed very small in size, looking a little like a Boston terrier. He never quite took to people and was often snappy, and I always felt that so dire a trauma as a youngster affected him mentally.

Flat Chests

Sometimes breeders experience puppies that have very flat chests. The puppies lie flat out, almost in a prone, spread-eagled position. These pups frequently have difficulty in breathing and take short sharp gasps. One theory is that they have spent too much time lying on top of a heated mat but I have experienced this problem with litters that have been raised under overhead heated lamps. The best solution is to place a small pillow under the chest which helps to ease their breathing. I have had a fifty/fifty success rate at rearing pups in this condition.

Water Babies

This condition also happens with human babies. There is a theory that it is related to a zero-thyroid function in the foetus. Such puppies normally only live for a few minutes. These are also termed 'Anasarca' puppies: foetuses that do not drain fluid in the normal manner. They become water-filled, and are often two or three times the weight of a normal pup. It is impossible for these puppies to pass through the pelvic opening of the birth canal, so a Caesarean is necessary. Unfortunately, their occurrence is difficult to predict, even with the ultrascan.

Deformities

Bulldog puppies often have strange, misshapen hind legs that turn round and face the opposite way. This is a common deformity, caused while the pup is packed inside the womb. The condition will begin to right itself within a few days. Many a good pup has been put down to sleep by vets that have mistakenly considered them to be deformed.

Any deformity of the front legs is a different matter.

In some puppies the sexual organs are deformed, unfinished or of ambiguous gender. Your vet will check for this.

Colic

If a Bulldog puppy cries out when you touch it, colic may be the cause. Gas builds up

A five-week-old puppy ready for lunch. (Photo: Simon Lathan.)

163

in the stomach as the puppy either overeats or swallows air while bottle feeding. If the entire litter has colic it is probably that the bitch's milk is being affected by antibiotics. Sodium bicarbonate in either powder or tablet form in the bitch's drinking water often helps, although as a result you will find that both the bitch's and the puppies' motions are loose.

Dehydration

If a puppy appears lethargic or lazy, pinch the skin at the top of the neck. It should spring back as you release it; if it returns slowly the puppy is dehydrating. The urine will start to concentrate and darken in colour; constipation will set in and the puppy will strain to pass hard, round faeces as its system becomes increasingly toxic. The puppy should be given an electrolyte such as Lectade powder, obtainable from your vet and easily dissolved in fluid. Administer every half hour at first, lengthening the time as the patient improves. This will rehydrate the puppy and assist in flushing out its system.

Diarrhoea

Always a bad sign, diarrhoea goes cap in hand with undersized, weak, sickly puppies. It is often caused by infection but it also occurs when food is not digested properly. Frothy, bad-smelling diarrhoea usually means an *E. coli* infection. Cut down on the milk feeds and administer half-strength electrolyte solution, gradually reintroducing milk as the condition improves. If the puppy shows no improvement after a day, contact your vet who will probably suggest antibiotics.

Antibiotics

The intestine teems with millions of different bacteria that protect us against infection and help our digestive systems to function smoothly. Puppies born in the sterile environment of the womb are born bacteria-free and feed on mother's milk, which is also bacteria-free. It is for this reason that there is no odour from their excrement, and mother is quite happy to clean them herself. As time goes on, say after weaning, this will all change. New bacteria grow in the puppies' guts, odours will begin to develop, and the bitch may become reluctant to clean them.

From the moment of birth, puppies will begin to gather a selection of vital bacteria or gut flora. There are good and bad bacteria that continually wage war, with the good maintaining the status quo. Antibiotics are effective but indiscriminate: they wipe out the infection but kill the good bacteria at the same time. These good or 'Bio' bacteria are found in natural live yoghurt, which has been known to provide dramatic results when administered to seriously ill pups. This yoghurt is readily available at health-food shops, but make sure that it is not the flavoured type and that it has not been frozen.

Growth and Progress

The pups should be weighed each day, at the same time religiously. This is very important as it is the best way to monitor their steady progress, and any fluctuations will alert you if anything is going amiss. Remember, a newborn puppy may lose weight for the first day or so, and those being left behind may need extra supplementary feeding.

Eyes normally begin to open at around ten days. They will have a bluish hue about them, almost like a bloom, but this will clear as time goes on.

The first (deciduous or milk) teeth will start to erupt when the puppy is a couple of weeks old, and all the teeth will be present by the age of eight or nine weeks. Over the following four months or so, these teeth will gradually be replaced by the permanent ones. Occasionally, puppies will grow a permanent tooth while retaining the milk one; these retained milk teeth should be removed by the vet to allow the permanent one to develop properly.

Up on all Fours
Bulldog puppies will start by getting up on their front legs and propelling themselves with the rear. It is important that they have some form of exercise or pen area that has a reasonable grip to the surface. Shiny surfaces are easy to keep clean but are slippery, and give little or no traction for the inquisitive puppy.

By three weeks they should be starting to get up and about on all fours. Some take a lot longer than others to get up on their legs and occasionally we have what are termed as swimmers – puppies whose legs do not support them. You will need to speak to an experienced breeder on this point, but there is no reason why these puppies should not finish as normal active Bulldogs.

Weaning

Many breeders start weaning after two to three weeks. I usually prefer to wait until at least four weeks, when I start by scraping wafers of beef or sometime tinned or bottled baby food on to the end of my finger or teaspoon. You will be surprised how quickly and how much the puppy will eat at this first session. I will then begin to alternate with creamy, milky foods, such as tinned custard or creamed rice, soaked baby rusks, usually mixed with a drop of honey. Nearly all the major dog-food manufacturers now produce excellent puppy-weaning porridges that contain everything they could possibly need.

When you start weaning with the finely scraped minced beef, do not push the steak into the puppy's mouth. Let the puppy take it from you, a small pellet at a time. Do this once a day for the first few days, then increase to twice daily for the next couple of days. Try not to introduce too many different foods too quickly. After the mince, introduce baby rusks soaked in milk or milk substitute. If the puppies appear reluctant to lap straight away, use a small plastic spoon. Those used for human babies are ideal as they are more rounded than a teaspoon. Put this under their noses and the smell will encourage them to start lapping.

Once the puppies begin to lap, you can introduce other foods, such as tripe, scrambled eggs with grated cheese, finely chopped chicken and tinned puppy food. I aim to give around five or six meals a day, alternating milk and meat meals.

Start by dry-frying the mince steak, then add a small amount of gravy granules. When browned, add a cup of water to the mince. Last-ly, I grate cheese over each beef or chicken meal. At five or six weeks the weaned puppies will enjoy drinking evaporated milk, mixed half and half with water.

For the first couple of weeks of weaning I normally alternate feeding with mother. After the fourth week you will find that for no apparent reason the puppies will just go off milky feeds and show more interest in the meat ones.

Homes for the Puppies

It is the breeder's responsibility to find homes for the new puppies. By the time the puppies are weaned and ready to leave their dam, you will probably have a number of people, including perhaps the stud-dog owner, who are interested in buying one of them. Good, established breeders will usually have more homes than pups. However, you will want to satisfy yourself that any potential owners are able to provide the love and care that the puppies need. At the same time, the breeder must provide all the necessary information and paperwork (*see* Chapter 3), a diet sheet (*see* below), and any other advice that a new owner may require.

Diet Sheet

This is a typical diet for a puppy of seven to eight weeks:

Breakfast
Tripe or tinned puppy food mixed with a complete puppy food of your choice.

Lunch
Scrambled egg, made with a little butter and milk, mixed with grated cheese
or
Baby rusks soaked in milk.

Teatime
Chicken or fish, such as coley, mixed with soaked complete puppy food
or
Cooked minced beef mixed with soaked complete puppy food.

Supper
Tinned puppy food mixed with complete puppy food.

We often complement these meals with treats such as tinned, creamed-rice pudding, tinned custards, or semolina mixed with honey. If you are feeding a complete food with dry meat such as chicken, soak it first in a small amount of warm water. From ten to twelve weeks you can gradually start to reduce the number of feeds per day.

10

Ailments and Diseases

Many of the problems that might affect your dog can be avoided with good diet, correct exercise, and good general husbandry. This includes ensuring that your dog is regularly groomed, properly wormed, and has regular inoculation boosters, and that his bedding, and food and water bowls, are kept clean. As a rule, vigilance pays off: it is far better – and usually easier – to treat a condition or illness at its onset; delay can make treatment more complicated (and sometimes more expensive).

Weighing your Bulldog

Obesity is unhealthy in that it places undue stress not only on the limbs but on the vital organs. The Bulldog is by definition a solid, well-boned dog, but this is not the same as being fat. Care taken to provide a healthy diet and sensible exercise will prevent most problems, but if your dog is very overweight you can consult your vet for advice. On the other hand, weight loss can be symptomatic of a health problem, so if your Bulldog suddenly loses weight, consult your vet.

I find the best way to weigh a Bulldog is to hold him with one arm around the chest and the other supporting him from underneath. Then stand on the scales and subtract your weight from the reading.

Taking your Dog's Temperature

Your dog's temperature is the best indication of whether he is off colour. I dislike the glass and mercury thermometers, preferring to use one of the many new electronic digital types, easily obtainable from either your vet or high-street chemists.

The thermometer should be inserted carefully into the dog's rectum and the temperature read. The electronic type has the added advantages that it will bleep when the temperature has stabilized, and it will give the previous reading each time it is switched on, which is handy when regularly checking the patient's progress.

Normal temperature is 101.4°F (38.5°C). If a dog's temperature reaches 103°F (39.4°C) or above it is advisable to consult your vet. Bulldogs travelling in cars, possibly to the vets, can sometimes read up to two degrees fahrenheit higher than normal. Pregnant bitches will usually drop to 98°F (36.5°C) when whelping is imminent. A rise in temperature will usually accompany the waters breaking.

Painkillers

Painkillers should only ever be used under the direction of your vet. Do not be tempted to administer what you might consider to be fairly harmless remedies, such as aspirin, without your vet's advice.

The main painkillers used for dogs, normally for lameness and related injuries, are listed in degrees of strength: Aspirin, Paracetamol, Phenylbutazone, PLT (Prednoleucotropin), Finadyne and Metacam (sometimes administered as a one-off shot), Prednisitone (known sometimes to induce thirst, hunger and panting).

General Health Problems

Diarrhoea

For loose motions, use a Metronidazole-type preparation. For more serious runs, your vet will prescribe a stronger remedy. Change the dog's diet to boiled fish or chicken mixed with rice or scrambled egg. One of the side-effects of serious diarrhoea is dehydration, so it is important not to restrict your dog's access to water.

Diarrhoea can be caused simply by a sudden change in diet or by a dog's eating something to which his digestive system is unaccustomed. However, it is also a symptom of a number of other diseases and conditions, so if diarrhoea persists you must consult your vet. It is especially serious in puppies, when it can quickly result in a prolapse of the rectum.

Bad Breath

Halitosis becomes more pronounced as your Bulldog grows older. I use a scalpel-type instrument, which can be purchased at shows to descale the yellow tartar that builds up on teeth. If you are not confident about doing this, or if the gums seem inflamed, ask your vet for advice.

Anal-Gland Impaction

These glands, sometimes referred to as anal sacs, are positioned on either side of the internal sphincters. The glands secrete a viscous fluid that can be a light grey to brown colour, and vary from watery to paste-like in texture. There is a theory that the discharge gives off a charac-teristic scent for each individual dog. However, these sacs are not nec-essary for the modern domestic dog and they can be surgically removed if they become infected.

Bulldogs seldom suffer from impacted anal glands, less so if their diet contains the correct amount of roughage. The glands will auto-matically empty as the dog's motions are passed, but sometimes bac-teria or even segments of tapeworm can block ducts. The first signs that the glands may be impacted is your Bulldog dragging, or as it is termed 'scooting' his bottom along the floor and trying to lick or gnaw at his back legs.

Your vet will quickly and easily perform the task of emptying the glands. However, with a little practice you may wish to attempt the procedure yourself. Enlist the help of a friend or your partner to securely hold your Bulldog's head. Make sure that you are wearing either rubber or disposable gloves. Place a medium-sized piece of cot-ton wool or gauze or lint over the rectum, then, using the sides of your thumb and forefinger, squeeze firmly behind both sides of the anus. The glands will feel like two small eggs on either side and will quick-ly empty. Take care as the discharged fluid can squirt out at a fast rate and the smell can be quite noxious.

Nodding

Nodding sideways is usually a sign of a condition known as eclampsia (*see* Chapter 9), common in whelping bitches. However, uncontrolled nodding up and down, or shaking, is normally and indication of an ear infection, and veterinary help should be sought immediately.

Wet Eczema

This condition often starts as a small patch of wet, raw skin, more often than not on the neck. A visit to the vet will result in the prescription of

Ch. Honclo Sweet Clover, born 23 October 1983, and bred and owned by Pauline Horner. This picture was taken at the grand age of thirteen and a half years. (Photo: Simon Lathan.)

a tube of ointment and being told to return to the surgery in the next ten to fourteen days if the problem persists. It normally does persist, as the patient can't resist scratching, and in any case you will be treating the symptoms not the cause. Where the neck is affected, ear mites are usually the culprits. When I first experienced this problem in Bulldogs, I was advised to treat it with antibiotics and anti-bacterial powder. All this did was clog the coat up into a hard crust which, when the condition subsided, fell away to expose bare skin.

With any type of wet eczema, time is of the essence as a minuscule patch can develop into an area the size of a football within hours. My vet will administer an injection of antibiotics combined with a steroid to reduce inflammation. The rest is then up to you and your hard work. Literally scrub the infected area with a diluted antiseptic wash such as Hibiscrub, three to four times daily. Make sure that you thoroughly dry the area with paper towelling. As soon as any yellow-greenish bacteria start to appear, repeat the process. The vet will give you a course, probably of broad spectrum antibiotics to administer orally throughout the treatment. This really works and I have saved countless show dogs' coats.

Emergencies

Some illnesses may be quite serious, either in the long or short term, but there are others that must be termed emergencies because time is of the essence and the first priority is to get your dog to a vet. Apart from those affecting the whelping bitch (*see* Complications, Chapter 9), the most common emergencies are as follows.

Heatstroke

Heatstroke can be fatal, and it frequently surprises people how quickly a dog will succumb. While Bulldogs enjoy summer weather, they are susceptible to heatstroke, so the subject is covered in some detail in Chapter 5 (*see* page 95).

Poisoning

Always make sure that all medicines, canine or human, are kept safely in a secure cupboard. Rat or mouse poisons should never be put down in a house where there are pets. Warfarin, for example, which is the most widely used rat poison, is extremely palatable to dogs and can cause fatal haemorrhages. Most of the modern weedkillers have no antidote, and if taken are fatal to man as well as to dogs. Strychnine, a poison which causes terrible convulsions and death, is readily available to farmers who use it to poison moles.

If you know that your Bulldog has swallowed a poison, rather than absorbed it through the skin or pads, for example, immediately give him an emetic (substance to induce vomiting). The most handy everyday emetic is a really strong salt and water solution, given like a dose of medicine. Keep the dog warm and take him straight to the vet. Tell your vet quite clearly what type of poison you suspect.

Pyometra

Pyometra is a form of metritis which most commonly occurs in middle-aged maiden bitches up to nine weeks after a season, although it can occur after a first season. It is caused by an infection in the uterus which produces pus.

The symptoms include a marked thirst, loss of appetite, a rise in temperature, and general dullness or depression. In some cases, known as 'open pyometra', the pus will be discharged from the vagina. In 'closed pyometra' the pus is not discharged but instead builds up in the uterus, causing abdominal distension. This condition is an emergency, and veterinary help should be sought immediately. Most vets will perform a hysterectomy, although I have had two bitches recover with antibiotics and intravenous drips, and live to produce fine litters.

Shock

Shock may occur after any severe trauma. Typical causes of the trauma include injury, burns, stings, haemorrhage, surgery, and conditions such as heatstroke. Shock is a clinical condition in which blood supply to the vital organs is severely impaired. It is extremely serious in that it can in itself be fatal, whether or not the condition precipitating it might be considered to be so.

The chief symptoms of shock are: weakness, cold skin and extremities (feet, ears, etc.), pale gums, lips and eye rims, rapid, shallow breathing, weak pulse, and rapid heartbeat. The dog may also be unconscious. Shock requires immediate veterinary assistance, but on the way to the vet, or until the vet arrives, do the following: control any blood loss, lay the dog on his side with his head slightly lower than the rest of his body, and keep him warm.

Parasites

Parasites can be divided into two main categories: internal (endoparasites) and external (ectoparasites). As a rule, parasites can be kept under control quite simply. Once again, vigilance and good husbandry are what is needed.

Worms

Most dogs will at some time in their lives suffer from worm infestation, or at least ingest worm eggs or larvae. So as a matter of course your dog should be wormed regularly throughout his life, and not just when he is a puppy. Your vet will provide the most effective worming preparations; otherwise, standard wormers are available from pet shops. There are two main types of worm – roundworm and tapeworm – and various species of each.

The most commonly occurring roundworm (ascarid) is *Toxocara canis* (up to 8in/20cm long), which is primarily found in pregnant bitches and young puppies. It is passed from the bitch to the puppies first via the placenta, and then via her milk, which is why it is essential to follow a strict worming routine with pregnant and nursing bitches, and young puppies, although it is very important that this is done under the guidance of your vet.

There are various types of tapeworm, but the most commonly occurring ones are *Dipylidium caninum* (up to 20in/50cm long) and *Taenia Hydatigena* (up to 16ft/4.8m). The first is passed to the dog in larval form via the flea; the second is contracted from eating raw, infected offal. Neither is passed directly from dog to dog, as with all tapeworms, both consist of a number of segments (each of which contain eggs), which periodically break off at the rear and then pass out of the body where they are visible in the faeces.

Nowadays, the vet will worm your dog with a combined wormer that is effective against both tapeworm and roundworm.

Fleas

Many owners are embarrassed to admit that their Bulldog may occasionally have fleas, rather like the schoolboy who is sent home from school with head lice. However, fleas are extremely common, especially in the summer, and most dogs – pedigree or other – will pick them up at some stage. The most important thing is to act quickly because quite aside from the discomfort they may cause to the dog, flea infestation can trigger an allergic reaction or other skin problems such as eczema. It should also be remembered that the flea is the intermediate host of the *Dipylidium* tapeworm, so control of the former is important in the prevention of the latter.

Fleas live by feeding on the dog's blood, which they extract by first biting into the skin, usually causing intense irritation. The most common flea-bite sites are on the insides of the upper legs, around the tail, and behind the ears. Fleas are darkish-brown in colour, although you are most likely to notice their dark, sand-like droppings (especially on lighter-coated breeds), than the fleas themselves. However, the most obvious sign that your dog may be affected is that it frequently scratches itself.

In warm weather, the flea's life-cycle is about fifteen days, during which time the female will lay up to 500 eggs in the dog's bedding, in cracks in the flooring, and in carpets and any other soft furnishings. This is why it is essential to treat both the dog and his environment when eradicating fleas.

Very effective environmental sprays are available from your vet or local pet shop, and parasitical shampoos or powder soon eradicate fleas in the dog's coat. A second blitz is always necessary as many of the flea larvae will not have hatched during the first application.

The latest flea collars are most effective, although a Bulldog is likely to remove the collar before you have time to turn your back.

Ticks

Ticks are commonly picked up by your Bulldog when walking in rural areas frequented by cattle or sheep; in less rural areas, dogs may occasionally pick up hedgehog ticks.

The tick climbs on to the dog and then, usually, makes its way up to the neck or chest area where it firmly attaches itself to the dog by burying its mouthparts in the skin. At this early stage the tick is small and inconspicuous, but as it becomes engorged with blood it swells until it is eventually the size of a pea; it then appears like a wart-like, pale or beige lump. When it is fully engorged, it will usually release its grip and fall to the ground, but the process can take days.

Some ticks carry diseases that can then affect their hosts, so it is important to remove a tick as soon as it is found. However, a tick's grip is extremely powerful, so do not attempt to dislodge it without first applying a spirit-based substance (such as alcohol, petrol, petroleum jelly, surgical spirit) to encourage it to loosen its hold. It can then be carefully extracted with a pair of tweezers by twisting it away in an anti clockwise direction. It is very important to make sure that no part of the tick is left embedded in the skin as this can cause serious infection. If you are not quite confident of successfully removing the tick, consult your vet.

Lice

Lice occur less frequently than fleas and ticks, but where they do they can cause irritation and other related skin problems.

Lice are small, slow-moving, whitish or pale-orange insects. They spend their entire life-cycle on the dog, where they extract blood by biting or sucking. The female louse lays the eggs near the base of the hairs. Lice are passed directly from one dog to another, so it is important to treat all dogs that may have come into contact with the affected dog. Specialist shampoos are effective in killing lice, although more than one application may be necessary to ensure complete eradication.

Mange

Mange is a condition caused by microscopically small mites that live in the skin. There are two types of mange: sarcoptic and demodectic. Both must be diagnosed from skin scrapings taken by the vet.

Sarcoptic mange is highly contagious and occurs most frequently but not exclusively in young dogs. It tends to affect the muzzle and ear flaps first and then spreads backwards. It causes intense irritation, and the dog's consequent scratching results in baldness and inflammation of the affected areas; in severe cases it will cause general unthriftiness. In any case you will need assistance from your vet, who will be able to prescribe an emulsifiable concentrate containing phosmet, which should be sponged on to the skin. Rubber gloves should be worn for this, and the procedure repeated daily for about fourteen days (or as your vet directs). In some cases, antibiotics may also be necessary.

Demodectic mange is a less common, but far more serious form in that acute cases can cause toxaemia. It is not contagious; instead, the mite is congenitally acquired from the dam and appears to remain harmlessly present in very small numbers in most dogs. When it does flare up – perhaps as a result of a weakened immune system – it occurs in young dogs of less than a year old, and it primarily affects the face and legs where it causes hair loss, and either greasy or scaly skin, accompanied by an unpleasant smell. Unlike sarcoptic mange, the disease does not cause irritation until it is well advanced. Treatment is notoriously difficult and too often ineffective. In very severe cases, the resulting debilitation, distress and secondary complications are such that euthanasia is the kindest solution.

Infectious Diseases

The most serious canine infectious diseases are: distemper (known as 'hard pad'); leptospirosis (two forms); infectious canine hepatitis (CAV-1); canine parvovirus (CPV-1 and CPV-2); canine parainfluenza virus; and rabies. Protection against the first four diseases is included in the combined vaccine given to your dog when he is a puppy (*see* Chapter 3), and in subsequent boosters throughout his life. The rabies vaccine is not included in the standard inoculations, and is only given to dogs that are being exported.

Kennel cough is one other highly infectious disease. There are a number of viral causes, the main one being the group of *Bordatella*

176

viruses. *Bordatella* can be specifically vaccinated against, but this is not usually done unless your dog will be staying in boarding kennels.

Hereditary Defects

There are a number of conditions or defects that have no direct physical cause. Rather they are passed genetically from one generation to the next. Genetic inheritance of defects is quite complicated, which means that in many cases a dog can carry a defect without its ever becoming physically apparent; he may, however, pass the defect to his offspring in whom it may manifest itself (*see* Chapter 8). A few conditions are not genetically inherited but are nonetheless congenital: these include roundworm infestation and demodectic mange.

'Cherry Eye'

Unlike man, the dog has a third eyelid, or 'nictitating membrane', situated in the inner corner of the eye. Behind this is pinkish tissue called the Hardarian gland. 'Cherry eye' is the prolapse of this gland, which then protrudes from behind the third eyelid, appearing like a cherry in the corner of the eye.

The condition is becoming increasingly common in Bulldogs; and the chances are that if one cherry pops out, the other will shortly follow. This is worth bearing in mind if your vet prefers to remove the gland under a general anaesthetic, in that it may make sense to remove both as a cautionary measure. The gland can also be removed under a local anaesthetic. Some maintain that the removal of the gland results in drying of the eye, but I have not experienced such a case in any of my Bulldogs that have undergone surgery.

Elongated Soft Palate

This congenital condition affects the breed far less now than when I bought my first Bulldog in the mid-1970s. Not only will it impair the dog's ability to eat, but it will interfere with his breathing. Generally he will regurgitate, or bring up, his food, often several times before he manages to digest it.

The condition will possibly need corrective surgery. Naturally, any dog that has suffered with soft palate should never be used as breeding stock.

Entropion and Ectropion

These conditions affect the eyelids of the dog. With entropion, either the top or bottom eyelids, or sometimes both, turn inwards, and as a consequence the lashes rub continually on the eyeball, causing irritation and weeping. The condition may need corrective surgery but often, if there are only a few offending hairs, a skilful vet will manage to remove them with tweezers. Ectropion is the reverse of the entropion in that the eyelids turn outwards, rather than in, and cause the lower lid to gape and cause the haw to show.

Hips

Bulldogs' hip sockets are very shallow and most dogs, if turned upside down, can easily click the joints in and out. As Bulldogs mature they muscle up, and few then experience problems with their back end. If they appear unsteady, this will normally right itself with short regular exercise. After all, Bulldogs skim, not drive, from behind.

Prolapsed or Narrow Trachea

This is a problem that seems to be on the increase. One train of thought is that as the puppy grows, his trachea does not keep up with the rest of his fast-developing body. This causes a restriction of breathing. It can eventually right itself, although the strain on the trachea can lead to an eventual prolapse and this is inoperable. If you suspect that your Bulldog has this problem, consult your vet and the breeder.

Holistic Medicine

In recent years there has been a marked change in people's approach to health and medicine. Many have turned to holistic, or complementary, medicine with successful results. Interest in homoeopathy is doubling every five years, and there is a steady increase in the use of acupuncture, and other healing methods such as 'the laying on of hands' in which the healer's energy is used to unblock and strengthen the healing energy in the patient.

The principle behind holistic medicine is the treatment of the patient as a whole, rather than merely prescribing against the symptoms of a disease. The best-known alternative healing methods probably include homoeopathy, herbalism, acupuncture, aromatherapy, and healing. There are many others: even diet is a form of medicine – but all have in common the utilization of the body's own energy to trigger its innate healing force.

There is a common misconception that all complementary medicines are innocuous and can therefore be prescribed or taken without care. As with all medicines, remedies should be treated with respect and used in accordance with instructions. If you wish to contact a vet who will prescribe homoeopathic medicines, write to the British Homoeopathic Association (*see* Useful Addresses). The association is a charitable foundation, so enclose a stamped addressed envelope and they will send you an information pack.

Commonly Used Remedies

The following is a list of various homoeopathic and herbal remedies, along with a few dietary supplements, which are frequently used to treat common ailments or improve general condition.

Aconite
This is a useful treatment for shock.

Apis-Mel
A homoeopathic remedy used in the treatment of stings and swellings.

Arnica
This helps to relieve bruising, but it has also been found to be very effective in dogs suffering from panic attacks.

Bach Flower Remedies
These remedies, developed this century by Edward Bach, work well for both people and their pets. Rather than treating the disease, the remedies treat the state of mind, whose effect on healing process is now acknowledged to be very important. The most well known of Dr Bach's remedies is probably Rescue Remedy, which is a combined remedy useful in first-aid for treating a person or animal suffering from injury or other trauma.

Echinacea
Perhaps the best-known natural remedy to boost the immune system available in either tincture or tablet form. There is now overwhelming

evidence that *Echinacea* stimulates white-cell function and can be safely given to both puppies and adults. It is excellent for animals under stress, which is always a serious threat to the immune system.

Elderberry and Nettle
Rich in iodine and iron, these help to improve pigmentation and coat condition.

English Green Leaf and Celery Seeds
Well known for their use in the relief of rheumatism and arthritis, these are mild diuretics that reduce acid in the system and regulate acid–alkaline balance. They are effective in the treatment of bladder and kidney disorders including cystitus and incontinence.

Euphrasia
This is used to treat watery, inflamed eyes, and runny noses.

Evening Primrose Oil
This assists in the correction of hormone imbalances. It stimulates coat growth and skin recovery after a moult or excessive hair loss.

Eyebright
A herb that is used diluted in water, and often combined with other medication, in the treatment of dry-eye. It helps to cut down on the production of mucus, and is useful for dealing with conjunctivitis and allergies.

Garlic
A traditional herbal remedy for relief of coughs and upper respiratory conditions. It is good for general health and is a natural preventative for internal and external parasites such as worms and fleas.

Garlic and Fenugreek
Bulldogs perspire through their feet, and this sometimes leads to painful and unsightly interdigital cysts. The old tried and tested remedy for this and the cracking of pads was to bathe the feet and apply zinc and castor-oil cream, which only temporarily eased the problem. Garlic and fenugreek is an effective treatment. Recommended dosage is one tablet per 11–22lb (5–10kg) bodyweight. During the summer months, when the dog's feet perspire more, he will benefit from two tablets twice daily. Not only will the cysts clear up within a couple of

weeks, but it will prevent recurrence and improve the general condition of the dog's coat and skin.

Kelp Seaweed
A good mineral supplement effective in the treatment of obesity. It also improves coat growth and pigmentation, but be careful of using it in the summer months on dogs prone to skin problems associated with overheating.

Live Yoghurt
Small portions of live, not natural or flavoured fruit, yoghurt harbour friendly bugs that replace those killed off in the digestive tracts by antibiotics. Adding a little honey to the yoghurt will make it more palatable.

Malted Kelp
A useful remedy to stimulate the appetite of poor feeders, helping them to increase weight and regain lost condition. The addition of malt makes it ideal for bitches with young, for convalescing dogs and poor eaters, assisting in balancing metabolism. It also helps coat growth and pigmentation.

Raspberry Leaf
This is useful for problems associated with whelping, and it is effective in the prevention of phantom pregnancy. When used for whelping, continue to administer for a further week to ensure complete removal of afterbirth.

Rhus-Tox
Homoeopathic remedy for sprains, falls and general tissue injury.

Royal Jelly
A product of honey bees that many believe helps in reversing the ageing process in humans. I have received good reports on its use with nervous Bulldogs.

Ruta-Graw
A useful treatment for sprained tendons.

Senna Leaf, Cascara, Valerian Root and Dandelion Root
These are all gentle laxatives.

181

Skullcap and Valeria
These calm and relax dogs susceptible to hyperactivity, excitability and phobias. They will not cause drowsiness or impair normal behaviour, so they are ideal for travelling and training, and while in the showring. They are used in the control of epilepsy.

Slippery Elm and White Poplar Bark
These are for poor digestion; they increase the dog's tolerance of various foods, and when mixed with live yoghurt or skimmed milk they treat chronic diarrhoea.

St John's Wort
Mood altering natural tranquillizer.

Sunflower Oil
Many Bulldog owners give a teaspoonful of sunflower oil spread each day, accompanied by a garlic tablet which acts as a very efficient natural internal antiseptic.

Tea-Tree Oil
A great healer for skin problems but refrain from using if there are any signs of pus or infection. It is such an effective healer that it has been known to heal skin over the top of bacteria. It is also known to repel insects.

Wheatgerm Oil
This maintains fertility in both sexes.

11

Bulldogs Worldwide

United States of America

According to American Kennel Club records, the first Bulldog to be exhibited in America was Donald, owned by Sir William Verner. He was a brindle and white dog, weighing no more than 40 pounds (18kg). He was whelped in 1875 by Alpha out of Vixen, and he was exhibited at a New York show in 1880. The first Bulldog to attain his championship in the USA was Robinson Crusoe, who became a champion in 1888. C. G. Hopton, with his Ch. L'Ambassadeur, was the first in the USA to breed an American champion. The Standard used by the Bulldog Club of England was originally adopted as the American Standard. However, exhibitors felt that this standard was not concise enough, so in 1894 a committee was formed to develop an American Standard. In 1896, a few changes were made, and the Standard was adopted as it is known today. (The only change was made in 1975 when disqualification of Brown or Liver-coloured nose was added).

From the 1880s onwards, several well-known Bulldogs were imported from the United Kingdom. These included Harper (a son of Ch. British

Ch. Vardona Frosty Snowman, handled by his breeder and owner the late Dr Edward M. Vardon, wins BOB at The Bulldog Club of Indiana Specialty Show in 1961. Snowman, an all-white dog, sired fourteen champions. Dr Vardon's kennel achieved five consecutive BOB wins at the National Bulldog Club of America, and died in 1971 after 40 years in the breed.

183

The Detroit Bulldog Club held their 50th Anniversary Show in 1978. Judge Charles T. Nelson awards the 14-carat-gold medallion for Best of Breed to Ch. Smasher's Constant Comment, handled by Karl Foerster and co-owned by Ray Knudson of Kenosha, Wisconsin. Today, Ray is the editor of the Bulldog Club of America's magazine The Bulldogger. *Detroit Bulldog Club President, Joseph Collin's presents the trophy.*

Monarch), Graven Image and Holy Terror. Others were Sheriff, Princess Venn and Baron Killarney. Many prominent Bulldog breeders came to the fore such as J. P. Barnard, Frank F. Dole, Sam Green, W. B. North, E. Sheffield-Porter and John Cole. Around 1896, the Don Salano strain, known for producing low cobby specimens of the breed, became popular on both sides of the 'pond', producing winning dogs such as Dandy Venn, Orient Don, and Pleasant. In 1897 several more good dogs were imported, such as Pressmoor Force, His Lordship, Don Juan, Baron Stockwell and Silver King.

Imports were by now coming in fast and furious. Richard Croker caused a sensation at this time by importing the famous British Ch. Rodney Stone, purchased from Walter Jefferies for the unheard of sum of $5,000. Next he was to import Ch. Bromley Crib, again purchased for the fabulous sum of $4,000. All this was to pale into insignificance though when Thomas Lawson purchased the champion bitch La Roche for an incredible $6,000.

During the 1950s, the top Bulldogs were Ch. Kippax Dreadnought and Ch. Kippax Fearnought. The late 1950s and early 1960s brought Ch. Vardona's Frosty Snowman with Ch. Marinebull's All The Way dominating the 1970s. The top dogs of the 1980s

Ch. Taurus Trailblazer, by Ch. Steamboat of Killarney out of Aries Annie Oakly, owned by Abe and Suzie Segal.

The celebrated Ch. Millcoats Titus at the age of nine months winning his first speciality under judge Harry Deutsch. Titus became one of the country's most prominent winners and prolific sires. Owned by Duwane and Caroline Miller.

were led by Ch. Cherokee Yancey. In the 1990s, ten dogs have been ranked in the Top Ten Bulldogs in the United States for at least one year during their show careers. These dogs are Jean and Robert Hetherington's Ch. Hetherbull Bounty's Frigate; Caroline and Duwane Miller's Ch. Mill-coat's Titus; Mary Brunk's Ch. Rudyk's Louie Louie; Brenda and Robert Newcomb's Desert Victory; Ch. Prestwick Gawain owned by Robert Church, June Sickle and Cody Sickle. Cody has judged Bulldogs at Championship shows in the United Kingdom. Ch. Cherokee Daniel Boone, also owned by Cody Sickle; Ch. T-Town's Mr Jazz Man owned by Kimberley, Robert and Sandra Walter; Bliss and Bliss Ann Bancroft's Ch. Hetherbull Arrogant Ronald; Ch. Sandy Ridge Maj Ashley Wilkes owned by W. L. Carter; and Ch. Wencar Silver Flame owned by Beth and Phil Handrick. Silver Flame was bred in the UK by Carol and Ron Newman and was the first English import to break into the Top Ten in many decades.

The Bulldog Club of America

Although Bulldogs had been imported and shown in the United States since 1880, there had not been an organized breed club. On 1 April 1890, a

Ch. Hetherbull Arrogant George (Ch. Hetherbull Bounty's Frigate out of Hetherbull Arrogant Venus). Co-owned with H. Jack and Mickie Brown and one of the countless champions bred by Jean and Robert Hetherington, Jr.

Ch. Rudyk's Louie Louie (Ch. Rudyk's Little Augie out of Ch. Rudyk's Golden Crunch). Bred by Randy and Donna Rudyk and owned by Mike and Mary Brunk.

group of Bulldog fanciers met for the first time at the Mechanics Hall, Boston, to form what was to become the Bulldog Club of America (BCA). Mr H. D. Kendall, of Lowell, Massachusetts, conceived the idea of forming an organization for 'the purpose of encouraging the thoughtful and careful breeding of the English Bulldog in America, to perpetuate the purity of the strain, to improve the quality of native stock, and remove the undesirable prejudice that existed in the public mind against the most admirable breed.'

In 1904 the BCA's constitution and byelaws were amended, the club became incorporated, and it was recognized by the American Kennel Club as the parent club for all Bulldog speciality clubs.

The Bulldog Club of America has grown: membership numbered 2,864 in 1997. There are fifty-seven BCA member speciality clubs across the country. During 1997 they sponsored sixty-six Bulldog speciality shows, in addition to the speciality shows hosted by each of the eight BCA geographical divisions and the annual Bulldog Club of America National Show.

The club has five national

The famous Ch. T-Town's Mr Jazz Man, awarded over 100 Best of Breed wins and a multiple Group and Best in Show winner. Bred and owned by Robert and Sandra Walter, Toledo, Ohio.

Ch. Prestwick Gawain winning Best of Breed at the most prestigious of Bulldog gatherings, the Bulldog Club of America National Speciality, 7 September 1994. He was by Ch. Cherokee Lord Prestwick out of Ch. Jo-Bob's Duchess of Prestwick. Handled by Cody Sickle and co-owned with June Sickle and Robert Church, and bred by Robert and Marla Church.

officers: president, vice-president, secretary, treasurer, and AKC (American Kennel Club) delegate. Then there is a committee in charge of the various departments. The national club is divided into eight separate divisions, each with its own secretary (*see* Useful Addresses).

Registrations and Rankings

The American Kennel Club (AKC) registered 4,937 Bulldog litters and 13,673 individual Bulldogs during 1997. During the same year 246 Bulldogs completed their American Kennel Club championships and gained their titles. The AKC Club has a Gallery of National Winners, which consists of a collection of specially commissioned oil paintings.

At the end of each year the AKC publishes a list of the top ten ranking Bulldogs (the 1997 list is reproduced below). You will notice that they also list a tally of all the Bulldogs that they 'defeated' in their quest to achieve top-ten status, something that is not done in the UK and most European countries.

Ch. Mugshot's Standing Ovation, son of the celebrated Ch. Millcoats Titus out of Ch. Hailey's Comment. Owned and bred by Rick and Bridget Higginbottom.

187

Ch. Wimsey's Shrewsbury Gaudy. Presented here by Norma Gibson and owned and bred by Phil and Beth Handrick. 'Shrew' was the couple's first homebred champion and 'finished' at 18 months in 15 shows.

1997 Final Rankings

For the following rankings, one point was credited for each Bulldog defeated by virtue of Best of Breed wins during 1997. The American Kennel Club has released these results for wins recorded from 1 January to 31 December 1997. The dog's name, breeder and owner are given. The number in the right-hand column indicates the number of dogs the listed dog defeated.

1.	Ch. Mugshot's Standing Ovation, R. and B. Higginbottom. (Chicago Park, CA.)	1,583
2.	Ch. Evergreen's Rawhide, B. Bancroft, B. Van Guilder. (Lakeville, MN.)	1,536
3.	Ch. Cherokee Dakota Robert, C. Sickle. (Merrick, NY.)	1,177
4.	Ch. Luv-A-Bull Sir Stanley, K. and J. Hood. (Lee's Summit. MO.)	1,073
5.	Ch. Bufords Ann Thunder Rolls, K. and B. Lindemoen. (Sunland, CA.)	765
6.	Ch. Roscoe's White Lighting, P. Cardenas. (Suisun City, CA.)	730
7.	Ch. Showbiz Menage's Ava Gadner, J. Fisher, R. Smith. (Redding, CT.)	669
8.	Ch. Cherokee Mardel Sage, C. Chambers, C. Sickle. (Indianapolis, IN.)	595
9.	Ch. Westmore's Irish Creme, D. and S. Moore. (Woodbridge, VA.)	581
10.	Ch. Edwards' Ace In The Hole, J. and L. Elliott. (Lancaster, OH.)	554

Australia

Australia is a continent so vast that dog showing often involves car journeys that take days, and flights that can take up to four hours at a time.

Victoria

The British Bulldog Club of Victoria is one of the oldest breed clubs in Australia, having been founded in 1914. The president Mr W. Ohehir, and his wife Hazel, have been involved with the breed for forty-four years.

Victoria's modern-day kennels include Mrs Lil Robinson's Avonmist, which has produced Australian champions Avonmist Holly, Avonmist Lucas and Avonist Tiana Lee. Pat and Anne Rutlidge, a mother and daughter team, have for the past fifteen years maintained one of the state's biggest kennels, their most noted winners being the mother and son duo, Aust. Ch. Bullibrook Paper Tiger and Aust. Ch. Bullibrook Philadelphia.

Neil Stone, David Crebbin and Eric Healy are partners in the Craigrossie kennel, which has been importing and showing Bulldogs for some twenty-five years. Most notable of these is Merriveen Sno Flint, Kingrock Mr Angus and Kelloe Smashin Spencer. A chance meeting and subsequent friendship with Saul and Edythe Schor in 1989 led to the importation of frozen semen from the Am Ch. Sundance Matador for their most famous bitch Ch. Ianedcell Punky Brewster, producing two bitch puppies. The kennel's most famous dog to date is Ch. Craigrossie Tommy Tucker, and the most recent champions being C. Craigrossie Finius Fog and his daughter Ianedcell Punky Brewster. This progressive kennel keeps in touch with other bulldog breeders on a worldwide basis.

Young kennels include Kay and Colin Kindred's promising young dog

Aust. Ch. Craigrossie Finius Fog, handled by his breeder Neil Stone.

189

Aust. Ch. Ianedcell Punky Brewster, owned and handled by David Crebin.

Keswood Passion, and David and Debbie Hobbs, who have just bred their first champion Yangerdook Stallone for their Yangerdook kennel.

South Australia

Although the state is one of the largest in area, it is the smallest in terms of population. The breed became popular again during the 1980s, largely owing to the efforts of the late George Prykryl, who worked to re-establish the rebirth of the South Australian Bulldog Club in 1989. He imported several dogs during this period and did much to improve the breed in Australia.

During the 1990s, the state's shows have been dominated by a number of grand, consistently winning dogs, such as Ch. Allipundi Lord Harold, his brother Ch. Allipundi Lord Dexter, and Ch. Warfel Wolfman Jack, all shown by John and Maxine Cliff. There is also the four-times Best in Show winning Ch. Bulldogdom Liltusker, owned by Carol and Peter Sutton, and Ch. Elroston Lady Elanor, bred by Merl and Howard Randell and owned by Val Zachary and Jean Angel.

Faye and Dick Barry's Ch. Shyola Tuppenny Doll is the most well-known champion from the Shyola kennel, which has produced dogs such as Australian champions Shyola Dilla, Penelope and Aphelia. Amongst other accolades Tuppeny Doll won the spot at Australia's first Bulldog national under UK specialist Sheila Alcock.

Apart from those mentioned above, the larger kennels have by and large disappeared from South Australia.

Western Australia

The Western Australian club is relatively new but it is active through the efforts of Betty Killaby and an energetic committee. It was affiliated on 12 September 1991. The National Show was held here in Perth in 1997 and judged by UK's Anne Higginbottom (Tretun). Best in Show went to Brad Sinnatamby's Sinco Lil Marschapone with Aust. Ch. Fulbren Jovila Prinse as runner-up.

The major winning dogs of recent times in the state are Allana Dewaayer's Aust. Ch. Craigrossie Mons Poirot, Aust. Ch. Kingvan Thatcher, Brad Sinnatamby's Aust. Ch. Chajen Advocate, Aust. Ch. Btirbull King Dick, Ken Winter's Aust. Ch. Trybull Gipsy Princess, Dianne Noy's Aust. Ch. Noybull Mr Chaplan, and Aust. Ch. Noybull Gidgies Girl. Ken Winter is the current club president.

Tasmania

The state formed its own social club in 1981. The foundation member and club president was Mrs Kay Claridge. Since 1981, the club has sponsored its own Bulldog of the Year, and winners of this award have included Aust. Ch. Rosserta Blanca Star (owned by the Smith's Paseya kennels), Aust. Ch. Warrenglen Earl Haig (owned by the Chell's Warrenglen kennel), and Aust. Ch. Cairdeas Commander (owned by the Ingles Cairdeas kennel). Other winners have included Aust. Ch. Snobul Dream Maker (owned by the Chan's Snobul kennels) and Aust. Ch. Wholuvsha Banjo Best (owned and bred by Leanne and Maurice Contessi of the Forepaws kennel). Wholuvsha Banjo's Best is the only dog to have won on three consecutive years.

Since 1986, twenty-four new champions have been made up and over fifty litters have been recorded. In 1997 the club became affiliated to the Australian National Kennel Club (ANKC). Smith and Eberhardt's Paseya kennels have exported Bulldogs to Hawaii, and Paseya Rich Romance and Paseya Lova Million have both gained their American titles.

Several interstate breeders have made their homes in Tasmania, and these have included Brian and Helene Chell's Warrenglen kennel from Victoria, and Fred, Elfriede and Salina Chan's Snowbul kennel from New South Wales.

The Craigrossie kennel's lines have dominated the Tasmanian show scene of late, with Aust. Ch. Wholuvsha Banjo's Best (*see* above) winning runner-up at the 1995 National in South Australia. Though relative newcomers to the breed, Maurice and Leanne Contessi's Forpaws affix has produced other successful dogs such as Aust. Ch. Mountbest Hoop Dedoo, Aust. Ch. Forpaws Calamity Jane, and Forpaws Virtuosity.

191

New South Wales

This is the most highly populated state of Australia. The British Bull-dog Club of New South Wales began at the turn of the century as an amalgamation of two clubs. Its sister club, The Northern British Bull-dog Club, was formed in 1945 and now holds two championship shows.

Over the past seven years, the dogs of Glenn and Sharon Edmunds' Bratice kennel, seem to have taken the lion's share of winning with Aust. Ch. Buldawg Splash of Ice and then her three daughters Aust. Ch. Bratice That's Terrific, Aust. Ch. Bratice Splasha Dolla, and Aust. Ch. Bratice Splasha Colour. There has been a plethora of bitches winning Best in Shows, with That's Terrific taking sixteen Best in Shows (and nine times runner-up), and twenty-six Best in Groups. The afore-mentioned bitches have taken the CCs at the last six Sydney Royals and won Best of Breed on three occasions.

Another exhibitor and breeder that has risen to prominence over the last decade is Howard Randell, son of Meryl Randell of Elroston fame. Their biggest winner to date is Aust. Ch. Elroston Mr Sandman, the winner of thirty-eight Best in Shows. Howard has worked with, showed, and judged Bulldogs in the UK, as well as on the continent and in the United States. For a time he edited the well-known Ameri-can magazine *Sourmug* before returning to Australia. The Elroston ken-nel has made a big contribution to improving the gene pool, importing several dogs from the UK such as Aust. Ch. Ghezirah Bill Sykes whom I remember seeing, suckling as a baby at breeder Elaine Betts' home in deepest Surrey.

Dulcie Partridge of the famed Kama kennel has spent a lifetime, over sixty years, in the breed. She is a fountain of knowledge where the breed is concerned, and with her late husband Les bred many top champions.

Another successful kennel over the past eighteen years has been the Buldawg kennel, producing dogs such as Aust. Ch. Buldawg Butch Cassidy, Aust. Ch. Buldawg Make a Slash, and Aust. Ch. Sunsplasher. George and Elizabeth Hoewerth began breeding in 1976 and their Nonparell affix has produced such renowned dogs as Aust. Ch. Non-parell Lady Sarah, Nonparell Maggie Thatch, Nonparell Lay Leah, and Aust. Ch. Nonparell Miss Emmylou.

Queensland

The Queensland Bulldog Club, established in 1915, is the oldest dog club in the state.

The top-winning dogs over the past decade have included: Reg and Lorraine Collins's Aust. Ch. Reglor Lady Fergie and Aust. Ch. Reglor Lord Ferguson; Paul and Jennifer Brennan's Aust. Ch. Fullbren Jovila Prince; and Beverly O'Hara's Aust. Ch. Lyden Little Tom, Aust. Ch. Lyden Mr Football, Aust. Ch. Lyden Glamis, and Aust. Ch. Craigrossie The Oracle. Reg and Lorraine Collins are well-known judges and have supported the Queensland Bulldog Club for over twenty-five years. Jennifer Brennan is the current president and Andrew Morris, who has the Apmor kennel with his wife Pat, is the current secretary. Beverly O'Hara has been breeding and showing Bulldogs for some twenty-five years and her Little Tom took the National Show under South-African breed specialist Dave Frakes. Herb Field and until recently his late wife Joan, have bred and showed under their Saxondale prefix for over forty years.

Europe

As the Euro Note contributor for the Bulldog Club Inc. magazine *The Bulldog* I have been able to maintain close links with most of the prominent continental breeders. David McHale and I have judged on several occasions, awarding CACs and CACIBs in Norway, Sweden, Denmark, Germany, Italy, Spain, Portugal, the Netherlands, Hungary, Russia, Belgium as well as in the United Kingdom and the Irish and Czech Republics. Some countries, such as Italy and Spain, have seen not only dramatic improvements in the quality of the breed, but in the demand for it.

Spain

Spain is now the largest importer of Bulldogs from the United Kingdom, but the gulf between the top kennels of Dos Aguas and Blockhead and the other breeders appears to be widening with indiscriminate importation of Bulldogs, few if any compatible with breeders' existing stock.

People such as Peter Frantzen of the Dos Aguas affix and Anabel Molinas (Blockhead affix) have been particularly single-minded. Not only have they imported several carefully selected dogs from leading British Kennels, but have in many instances bred on and improved on these dogs.

193

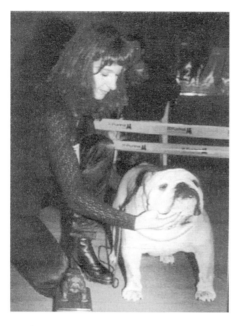

Anabel Molina handling her UK import Erindan Superboy of Hobtop, Top Bulldog in Spain 1997. With partner Louis Bernet, Anabel runs the highly successful Blockhead kennel.

Peter Frantzen has been one of the driving forces behind the sharp rise in the profile of the Bulldog Club of Spain. His Dos Aguas affix, taken from the name of a seventeenth-century ancestor, has been registered for over twenty years. One of his first imported dogs was Everso Umble of Ghezirah followed by Sandcroft Baloo of Kelloe, who notched up the titles of Spanish and International Champion and, in 1992, World Champion at Valencia.

Around this time, Peter purchased his foundation bitch who was to become his top-winning Sp. Eur. & Int. Ch. Kelloe British Pageant, litter-sister to Ch. Kelloe White Glove. She was twice European Champion, in 1993 and 1994, and all of her four puppies became Champions.

During 1997 this kennel won four of the eight Top Bulldog trophies: Top Junior Dog; Dos Aguas Nicholas; Top Bitch, Ch. Dos Aguas Jennifer; Top Stud, Ch. Dos Aguas Jacob; and Top Brood, Ch. Alki's Queen.

Anabel Molina Salas and Luis Bernet Perez's Blockhead kennels have made great advances in their showing and breeding programmes, importing such dogs as Ch. Ringablok Rudolph, and Ch. Erinden Superboy of Hobtop, who took the title of Top Bulldog in Spain during 1997. Other significant winners in 1997 were: Top Junior Bitch, Gina de Birfoo's Dog, and Top Puppy Bitch, La Chata After Karina.

Dos Aguas Nicholas, Top Spanish Junior Bulldog 1997.

194

Int. Euro. & World Ch. All To Love Sonny, handled by his breeder and owner Chiara Guria, one of Italy's leading breeders.

Italy

Italy has also seen the import of some exceptional dogs, although disappointingly some have not been allowed to fulfil their full potential in improving the overall quality of the breed because they have been sent on to other countries as soon as their show careers were completed.

Many Italian Bulldoggers regularly visit the UK's major shows. Riccardo and Chiara Guiria's celebrated dog Ch. All To Love Sonny swept the board throughout Europe, taking the European and World Champion titles. Paola Bonnetto has made a big impact on the Italian show scene with such top-winning stock as Ch. Bitter Sweet and Ch. Lion King di Hawkroad. Other new enthusiasts include Alfredo Sabatini and the Milan-based kennel of Franco Porta. Luciano Orsi still mantains a keen interest in the breed and is also a regular visitor to the UK.

Germany

Germany has introduced some

Italian enthusiast Dr Franco Porta handling his UK import Mymozo Victor Victorious for Kelloe. (BOB, Milan 1998.)

195

Germany. World Ch. Simplissimus Carlo sunbathing in style.

extremely tough legislation with regard to showing and breeding, causing the whole system to appear to collapse under its own weight. This has had a rather adverse effect on the general quality in the breed.

Petra Grell-Hansohm's Simplissimus kennel has been one of the most consistent kennels, producing such top-winning stock as World Ch. Simplissimus Carlo and the beautiful bitch Ch. Simplissimus Brigitte Bardot. Of the few kennels breeding to UK Standard, Uta Subert's Tenderfoot Bulls have had marked success with Ch. Tenderfoot Bulls Another Shakespeare, taking several Best in Shows including Berlin in 1997.

France

Helene Denis's du Quarrylane Cottage affix is probably the best known French affix, and her dogs have won virtually every title including Reserve Best in Show at the World Show in Amsterdam in 1985. In 1992, Bonifacio's Fernando of Sandean beat over 6,000 dogs to take Best in Show at Longchamp (the French Equivalent of Crufts).

The kennel started in 1978 when Helene acquired Nessie of Qualco. The six puppies that Nessie produced the following year represented a quarter of all bulldogs born that year in France. Helene became club secretary in 1984 and then president in 1992. She dedicates her time to judging and promoting the club, which now boasts a membership of 626 and a tally of puppies born in France in 1997 of 280, a remarkable feat.

The number of other champion owners and breeders include the following: M. T. Bertrand, Celine Bottussi, Rene Boudon, Michele Courvoisier, Malou Frank, Rene and Maryse Grandmougin, Lucien Grolleau, Denis Hindie, Chantel Julien, Izabelle and Joel Julou, Andre Leblon, Pascale Le Quilliec, Luciano Orsi, M. Pettillon, Corinne Poisson, Edwige Robart, Mme Roosenboom, Francis Rover, Charles Semser, Mme Simon and Roselyne Vandamme.

Netherlands

Anneke v.d. Maat's affix Tivoli Bulls was started in 1991 with the foundation bitch Bam-Bam of Lucky Yard. She produced C. Makepeace of the Tivoli Bulls and Cover Girl of the Tivoli Bulls. At the Dutch Clubshow in 1997 Bloody Mary of the Tivoli Bulls went Best in Show from a record entry of 226 Bulldogs. In 1993 the couple imported Isgraig Bendingo Boy, who was to become one of the most successful Bulldogs on the Continent, winning three Best in Shows and thirty-three CCs.

Other kennels of note are the Romakome's of Marij Koster, and Mrs A. van Wingerden's bitch, Bagheera v.h. Slaghek took the World title in Hungary in 1997.

Switzerland

The Swiss Club for English Bulldogs, formed in 1906 with fifteen founding members, was amongst the first of the breed clubs and, the eighth to become a member of the Swiss Kennel Club.

Over the past ten years, the highest number of Bulldogs

Netherlands. Anneke v.d. Maat handling Bloody Mary of the Tivoli Bulls, sired by Ch. Isgraig Bendingo Boy, out of Ch. Makepeace of the Tivoli Bulls.

197

bred and registered in Switzerland has been approximately seventy-five in any one year, but this is a small country with less than 7 million inhabitants. There are currently about 300 Bulldogs countrywide, and the Swiss Club for English Bulldogs has approximately 250 members.

After the Second World War, the Bulldog was practically nonexistent in the country until 1966, when Imelda Angehrn started breeding with two German imports and took the affix of Pickwick. Soon afterwards she imported the renowned Ch. Crossroads Calphurnia, pregnant to Ch. Walvra Red Ensign. Other high-quality Bulldogs imported by this kennel were Ch. Outdoors Humperdinck and Ch. Soldier Boy of the Regions. Imelda Angehrn is by far the major Bulldog breeder in Switzerland, if not the Continent, having bred some 280 litters and seventy home-bred champions.

In 1975, Evelyn Landis established her Goldengrove kennel. Since that time, she has bred over sixty litters and bred numerous champions including Goldengrove Lady Leandra, Goldengrove Quick-Step and Goldengrove Angara, who won the World Championship title in 1996 in Budapest, Hungary.

Another prominent breeder to emerge in Switzerland is Heidi Leibungut, who established her Goodbody's affix in 1992. Ch. Goodbody's Alistair has won numerous titles, including European Champion, Ger-

Japan. Kiyotaka Fujii handling one of his UK champion imports. His Kamanza Bulldog kennel has imported seven UK champions and done much to improve the standard of the breed in Japan.

198

man Federal Champion, and World Champion in 1994.

Switzerland holds three International Breed Shows annually, the most prestigious being the Bulldog Club Show which draws entries of more than 100 Bulldogs and exhibitors from as far afield as Austria, Germany, Holland, Italy and Spain.

Japan

Japan has many breeders that have run successful Bulldog kennels for decades. Not only is Japan one of the largest importers but it is one of the few countries where British and American stock jostles for top honours in the show ring.

Many of the established breeders include the Gold Star kennel of Tokuhiro Ikeda, Shigeru Tomono's Lucky Wave bulldogs, and Junji Iwama's Laughable Rock. Mr Iwama's impressive state-of-the-art purpose-built Bulldog kennel was an unforgettable experience. On the island of Fukuoka, Mr Kiyotaka Fujii has his Kamanza Bulldog kennel. Over the past sixteen years he has worked hard to improve the quality of Japanese-bred Bulldogs and to this end has imported seven UK champions, six of these males and three of these sons of Ch. Isgraig Red Baron.

Ch. Kelloe Truly Madly Deeply, bred by the author and David McHale, and owned by Kiyotaka Fujii in Fukuoka, Japan. A powerful, yet feminine bitch.

Appendix 1

Crufts Winners

The following is a list of all the Bulldog winners (dogs and bitches), since 1891. At this time, six points were needed for a dog to become a champion, but since Crufts was not a particularly large show in its early years, only one point was on offer for a win. You will also notice that between 1896 and 1898, Bulldogs were classified separately according to weight. D denotes Best Dog; B denotes Best Bitch.

1891
   Challenge Class (1 point): D – Ch. Bedgebury Lion.
   Challenge Class (1 point): B – Ch. Dryad.
1892
   Challenge Class (1 point): D – Ch. Bedgebury Lion.
1893
   No championship prizes.
   Challenge Class: D – Ch. Bedgebury Lion.
   Challenge Class: B – Ch. Dryad.
1894
   No championship prizes.
   Class open: D – Ch. Ch. Dockleaf.
   Class open: B – Magic.
1895
   No championship prizes.
   Class open: D – Ch. Monkey Brand.
   Class open: B – Ch. Bicester Beauty.
1896
   No championship prizes.
   Open Class (55lb and over): D – Guido.
   Open Class (45lb and over): B – Heavenly Pleasure.
   Open Class (45–55lb): D – Smart's Punch.

Open Class (35–45lb): B – Ch. Blackwall Beauty.
Open Class (under 45lb): D – Ch. Dimboola.
Open Class (under 35lb): B – Aston Noram.
1897
No championship certificates.
Open Class (over 55lb): D – Lord Francis.
Open Class (over 45lb): B – Charley's Aunt.
Open Class (45–55lb): D – Queer Street.
Open Class (35–45lb): B – Ch. Blackberry.
Open Class (under 45lb): D – Ch. Dimboola.
Open Class (under 35lb): B – Fantine.
1898
D – Ch. Boaz. B – Ch. Bicester Beauty.
1899
D – Ch. Baron Sedgemere. B – Ch. Blackberry.
1900
D – Ch. Bromley Crib. B – Ch. Battledora.
1901
D – Ch. Portland. B – Ch. La Roche.
1902
D – Ch. Prince Albert. B – Ch. Sweet Saint.
1903
D – Ch. Felton Prince. B – Ch. Felton Duchess.
1904
D – Ch. Heath Baronet. B – Ch. Cribette.
1905
D – Ch. Regal Stone. B – Ch. Woodcote Sally Lunn.
1906
D – Ch. Nuthurst Doctor. B – Ch. Buddug.
1907
D – Ch. Probang. B – Ch. Baroness of Teesdale.
1908
D – Ch. Chineham Young Jack. B – Ch. Silent Duchess.
1909
D – Ch. Chineham Young Jack. B – Ch. Silent Duchess.
1910
D – Ch. Chineham Paradox. B – Ch. Deodora Delilah.
1911
D – Ch. Chineham Paradox. B – Chineham Maluma.
1912
D – Ch. Deodora Monarch. B – Ch. Felton Comet.

1913
D – Ch. Stockwell Mayor. B – Ch. Oak Nana.
1914
D – Ch. White Marquis. B – Ch. Oak Nana.
1915
D – Ch. Letchford Mason. B – Minster Daisy.
1916
D – Ch. Challenger. B – Kissbonny.
1917
D – Ch. At Last. B – Ch. Deodora Dorothy.
1921
D – Ch. Sweet September. B – Ch. Regia.
1922
D – Ch. Jutland Jupiter. B – Ch. Regia.
1923
D – Ch. Caulfield Monarch. B – Ch. Regia.
1924
D – Ch. Caulfield Monarch. B – Ch. Meslisande.
1925
D – Ch. Dunscar Draftsman. B – Ch. Tufnell Launtett.
1926
D – Ch. Oakville Supreme. B – Ch. Hefty Barbara.
1927
D – Ch. Dominion Fortitude. B – Ch. Dame Daggers.
1928
D – Ch. Nizam of Woodhouse. B – Ch. Dame's Double.
1929
D – Ch. Tottonian Monarch. B – Ch. Dame's Double.
1930
D – Ch. Nizam of Woodhouse. B – Ch. Dame's Double.
1931
D – Ch. Pugilist. B – Ch. Rolls Rose.
1932
D – Ch. Crewe So Solarium. B – Ch. Brooklands Maze.
1933
D – Ch. My Lord Bill. B – Ch. Mountain Lassie.
1934
D – *Ch. Jasperdin of Din. B – Ch. Cloverley Brightstar.
1935
D – *Ch. Vindex Vistar. B – Ch. Basford Starturn.

1936

D – *Ch. Dinilo of Din. B – Ch. Boo Boo of Din.

1937

D – *Ch. Basford Revival's Replica. B – Ch. Cefnmabley Queen.

1938

D – Ch. Son O'Boomerang's Replica. B – Ch. Cloverley Blissful.

1939

D – *Ch. Son O'Boomerang's Replica. B – Ch. Bosworth Queen.

1948

D – Ch. John Blockbuster. B – Ch. Cheetham's Pride.

1950

D – *Ch. Ritestok Robin Hood. B – Ch. Good Grain.

1951

D – *Ch. Ritestok Robin Hood. B – Ch. Dromeside Destiny.

1952

D – Ch. Leodride Beau Son. B – Ch. Noways Chuckles
(Best in Show).

1953

D – Ch. Auraelean Autocrat. B – Ch. Noways Chuckles.

1955

D – Ch. Milord of the Regions. B – *Ch. Noways Chuckles.

1956

D – Ch. Shevythorn Solo. B – *Ch. Noways Chuckles.

1957

D – Ch. Kippax Doublenought. B – Ch. Threethorne Honeylight.

1958

D – *Ch. Merchant of Venice. B – Ch. Fairtrough Penny.

1959

D – *Ch. Tarus Red Cloud. B – Ch. Eastgate Carousel.

1960

D – *Ch. Mellea Jamie. B – Ch. Leodride Poppet.

1961

D – *Ch. Outdoors Kippand.

B – Ch. Lamerit Cornflower of Wyngrove.

1962

D – *Ch. Blockbuster Best Bitter. B – Ch. Albermar Bonanza.

1963

D – Ch. Goulceby Craigatin Brave Boy. B – Ch. Walvra Cherie Gal.

1964

D – Dorrays Tornado. B – *Ch. Walvra Sans Souci.

1965

D – *Ch. Mellea Hesagenie. B – Ch. Drewand Delilah.

1966

D – Ch. Boohawk Jeddar. B – *Ch. Baytor Telstar (Reserve Group).

1967

D – *Ch. Toby Jug of Wyngrove. B – Ch. Outdoors Anna.

1968

D – *Ch. Walvra Red Ensign. B – Ch. Thydeal Little Audie.

1969

D – *Ch. Walvra Red Ensign (Reserve Group).
B – Ch. Holeyn Duchess.

1970

D – Ch. Walvra Red Ensign. B – *Ch. Broomwick Blythome
Bumble Bee (Reserve Group).

1971

D – Ch. Thydeal Relentless. B – *Ch. Broomwick Blythome
Bumble Bee.

1972

D – Ch. Allomdom Encounter. B – *Ch. Crossroads Chloe.

1973

D – Ch. Bryneatons Barbarian.
B – *Ch. Portfield So Small (Group winner).

1974

D – *Ch. Beechlyn Golden Nugget of Denbrough.
B – Edgewick Tamara.

1975

D – *Ch. Beechlyn Golden Nugget of Denbrough (Reserve Best
in Show). B – Ch. Jackath Stargazer.

1976

D – Ch. Thydeal Golden Wonder. B – *Ch. Bellum Premiere.

1977

D – *Ch. Aldridge Advent Gold. B – Ch. Bellum Premiere.

1978

D – Ch. Branstonia Super Sam.
B – *Ch. Aldridge Anemone (Group Winner).

1979

D – *Ch. Romeo of Thydeal. B – Ch. Atozed Fiona.

1980

D – *Ch. Outdoors Jubi Junior. B – Ch. Aldridge Anemone.

1981

D – *Ch. Towyvale The Minstrel. B – Ch. Merriveen Maybe Baby.

1982
D – *Ch. Tyegarth Jacob of Kelloe (Reserve Group).
B – Ch. Merriveen Tipsi Cola.

1983
D – *Ch. Weltor Jack of Diamonds at Jorona.
B – Ch. Merriveen Maybe Baby.

1984
D – *Ch. Stockbull Big Ben. B – Ch. Merriveen That's My Baby.

1985
D – *Coatesmar Watney Keg. B – Ch. Sandean Sophie's Baby.

1986
D – *Ch. Tyegarth Jacob of Kelloe (Reserve Best in Show).
B – Ch. Ocobo Snow Queen.

1987
D – *Ch. Piledriver Hold That Tiger.
B – Ch. Sandean Sophie's Baby.

1988
D – *Ch. Willsmere Solid Silver. B – Ch. Rollben Ma Baker.

1989
D – *Packapunch Our Boy Max. B – Ch. Sandean Sophie's Baby.

1990
D – Ch. Willsmere Solid Silver. B – *Ch. Sibley Modesty Blaize.

1991
D – Ch. Amurton Dirty Harry at Kingrock.
B – *Ch. Aldridge Avita.

1992
D – *Ch. Willsmere Solid Silver. B – Frymad Florence of Bohass.

1993
D – *Ch. Tretun Sam Wella at Kingrock. B – Mistletoe Blanche.

1994
D – Ch. Ocobo Royal Heritage of Britishpride. B – *Wildax Paris.

1995
D – Gwenstan King Bruno of Broadcourt.
B – *Hiising History in a Moment.

1996
D – *Ch. Medbull Gold Dust over Kelloe.
B – Ch. Berrybrook Born to Boogie.

1997
D – *Ch. Ocobo Tully. B – Ch. Kentee Kizzy of Outdoors.

An asterisk (*) preceding a dog's name indicates 'Best of Breed'.

Appendix 2

Bulldog of the Year Title Winners

Here follows a list of the winners of the Bulldog of the Year title since the title was first established in 1977. For each year, the name of the title winner is given in bold, followed by the names of the winner's sire and dam (in brackets), and then the winner's sex and date of birth. Then follows the names of the breeder and owner, and the name of the dog who won Best Opposite Sex. Finally the names of that year's judges are given, with each judge's affix given in brackets. (Information reproduced by courtesy of the Bulldog Club Incorporated.)

1977
Ch. Bellum Premiere (Ch. Harada Ben Pepperdine × Saucy Scarle). Bitch: 11 November 1974.
Breeder: John Driver MRCVS. *Owner*: John Driver and Wendy Phillips.
Best Opposite Sex: Ch. Kilbarchan's Lord Percy.
Judges: Claude Bannister (Thatchways), Marjorie Barnard (Noways), Arthur Westlake (Baytor).

1978

Ch. Outdoors Jubilant (Ch. Aldridge Advent Gold × Outdoors Sunshine). Dog: 23 August 1977.
Breeder/Owner: George and Dora Wakefield.
Best Opposite Sex: Ch. Bellum Premiere.
Judges: Les Lund (Qualco), Norman Pitts (Allomdom), Jack Cook (Jackath).

1979

Ch. Outdoors Jubi Junior (Ch. Outdoors Jubilant × Pollyanna of Outdoors). Dog: 13 October 1978.
Breeder/Owner: George and Dora Wakefield.
Judges: Marjorie Barnard (Noways), Les Thorpe (Tuffnuts), Ormsby Issard-Davis (Quickly).

1980

Ch. Eskaidee Baggage (Ch. Aldridge Advent Gold × Eskaidee Trollope). Bitch: 4 September 1978.
Breeder/Owner: George and Marguerite Cook.
Best Opposite Sex: Ch. Outdoors Jubi Junior.
Judges: Kath Cook (Jackath), George Parker (Of the Regions), Tom Horner (Tartary).

1981

Ch. Merriveen Maybe Baby (Merriveen Son of Satan × Kingrock My-Nora-Tee). Bitch: 6 March 1979.
Breeder: Chris Thomas. *Owner*: Pat Dellar.
Best Opposite Sex: Ch. Ocobo Skipper.
Judges: Jack Bateman (Daneham), Godfrey Evans (Bryneatons),
John Story (Minotaur).

1982

Ch. Weltor Jack of Diamonds of Jorona (Ch. Brumigum Stroller Boy of the Regions × Jorona Winter Jasmine). Dog: 8 June 1981.
Breeder: Peter and Leslie Rothwell.
Owner: John and Fiona Rowe.
Best Opposite Sex: Ch. Chappark Bossy Bee.
Judges: Jack Cook (Jackath), George Parker (Of the Regions), Norman Pitts (Allomdom).

1983

Ch. Stockbull Big Ben (Bowcrest Patton ×
Candy of Fulham).
Dog: 22 January 1981.
Breeder/Owner: Graham Payne.
Best Opposite Sex: Ch. Chappark Bossy Bee.
Judges: Ron Bowers (Bowcrest), Les Thorpe
(Tuffnuts), Tom Horner (Tartary).

1984

Ch. Tyegarth Jacob of Kelloe
(Ch. Merriveen Happy Daze ×
Tyegarth Gabrielle). Dog: 19 December 1979.
Breeder: Sheila Cartwright. *Owner*: Chris
Bruton and David McHale.
Judges: Dorothy Jones (Broomwick), Ralph
Chamber (Castizo), Norman Pitts
(Allomdom).

1985

Ch. Merriveen Halcyon Daze
(Ch. Merriveen Happy × Merriveen Pepsi
Cola). Dog: 20 August 1980.
Breeder/Owner: Pat Dellar.
Best Opposite Sex: Ch. Brenuth Brittania
of Kelloe.
Judges: Ada Pitts (Allomdom), Dorrie
Thorpe (Tuffnuts), Harold Hayball (Thydeal).

1986

Bullzaye Sandy McNab (Wencar Silver
Sonlight × Merriveen Jasmine).
Dog: 1 January 1985.
Breeder/Owner: Richard and Betty Cassidy.
Best Opposite Sex: Ch. Sandean's Sophie's Baby.
Judges: Jean and Godfrey Evans (Bryneatons),
Pat Dellar (Merriveen).

1987

Ch. Willsmere Solid Silver (Ch. Aldridge Avanti × Ch. Willsmere Naughty But Nice). Dog: 20 May 1986.
Breeder/Owner: Viv and Graham Williams.
Best Opposite Sex: Ch. Chappark Little Madam.
Judges: Norman Pitts (Allomdom), Anne Higginbottom (Tretun), Les Cotton (Aldridge).

1988

Ch. Willsmere Solid Silver (Ch. Aldridge Avanti × Ch. Willsmere Naughty But Nice). Dog: 20 May 1986.
Breeder/Owner: Viv and Graham Williams.
Judges: George Parker (Of the Regions), George Walsh (Atozed), John Davies (Dewrie).

1989

Ch. Storming Passion of Ocobo (Ch. Quintic Amos of Ocobo × Belire Skip 'n' Hop). Dog: 25 July 1986.
Breeder: Mrs Rich. *Owner*: Pat and Norman Davis.
Best Opposite Sex: Ch. Merriveen Magnolia.
Judges: Vera May (Walvra), Chris Thomas (Kingrock), Minnie Wearmouth (Holeyn).

1990

Ch. Audstan Svengali (Ch. Aldridge Avanti × Wallbren Little Pretender). Dog: 25 July 1986.
Breeder/Owner: Nina Boulton.
Best Opposite Sex: Ch. Merriveen Magnolia.
Judges: Carol Newman (Wencar), John Story (Minotaur), Tom Horner (Tartary).

1991

Ch. Willsmere Solid Silver (Ch. Aldridge Avanti × Ch. Willsmere Naughty But Nice). Dog: 20 May 1986.
Breeder/Owner: Viv and Graham Williams.
Best Opposite Sex: Ch. Tretun Miss Matilda.

Judges: Gwen Biddle (Gwenstan), Bob Wain (Bondabull),
Ann v.d. Heuvel (Beefeeters Bulls).

1992

Ch. Willsmere Solid Silver (Ch. Aldridge Avanti × Ch. Willsmere
Naughty But Nice). Dog: 20 May 1986.
Breeder/Owner: Viv and Graham Williams.
Best Opposite Sex: Ch. Bramor Tailer Maid.
Judges: Marge Spickernell (Elsmar), Ada Pitts (Allomdom),
Arthur Rowe (Rockytop).

1993

Ch. Brampton Red Joshua
(Ch. Isgraig Red Baron × Brampton Sugar Girl).
Dog: 3 November 1989.
Breeder/Owner: Angela and Terry Davison.
Best Opposite Sex: Ch. Kelloe White Glove.
Judges: Jim Adams (Leydud), Les Thorpe
(Tuffnuts), Pat Perkins (Quintic).

1994

Ch. Ocobo Tully (Bewley Anzac × Ocobo New Edition).
Dog: 25 October 1992.
Breeder/Owner: Pat Davis.
Best Opposite Sex: Ch. Kelloe White Glove.
Judges: Bob Haydock (Cabinteely), Dorrie Thorpe (Tuffnuts),
Noel Morgan (Ringablok).

1995

Ch. Outdoors Country Gent
(Outdoors Revival × Bonifacio's Nanette at
Outdoors). Dog: 22 August 1992.
Breeder/Owner: Brian Daws and Dora
Wakefield.
Best Opposite Sex: Ch. Kentee Kizzy at
Outdoors.
Judges: Viv Williams (Willsmere), Pat
Meredith (Ameredith), Bill Cartwright
(Brandywell).

1996

Ch. Ocobo Tully (Bewley Anzac × Ocobo New Edition). Dog: 25 October 1992.
Breeder/Owner: Pat Davis.
Best Opposite Sex: Ch. Isgraig Bella Vega.
Judges: Carol Newman (Wencar), Pat Dellar (Merriveen), Godfrey Evans (Bryneatons).

1997
Ch. Ocobo Tully (Bewley Anzac × Ocobo New Edition). Dog: 25 October 1992.
Breeder/Owner: Pat Davis.
Best Opposite Sex: Ch. Delrousher Fantasy Delight.
Judges: Geof Nicholls (Weavervale), Sheila Alcock (Chiansline), Les Lund (Qualco).

Appendix 3

The Top Winning Dogs

Each year, the canine press publishes the name of the overall top-winning dog in each breed. This is a list of the Top-winning Bulldogs from 1973 to 1997 (reproduced by courtesy of *Dog World*).

1973 Ch. Portfield So Small
1974 Ch. Beechlyn Golden Nugget of Denbrough
1975 Ch. Beechlyn Golden Nugget of Denbrough
1976 Ch. Aldridge Advent Gold
1977 Ch. Aldridge Advent Gold
1978 Ch. Aldridge Anemone
1979 Ch. Outdoors Jubi Junior
1980 Ch. Outdoors Jubi Junior
1981 Ch. Ch. Tyegarth Jacob of Kelloe
1982 Ch. Ch. Tyegarth Jacob of Kelloe
1983 Ch. Tyegarth Lucifer
1984 Ch. Sandean Sophie's Baby
1985 Ch. Ocobo Slightly Noble
1986 Ch. Sandean Sophie's Baby
1987 Ch. Quintic Amos of Ocobo
1988 Ch. Willsmere Solid Silver
1989 Ch. Storming Passion of Ocobo
1990 Ch. Tretun Miss Matilda
1991 Ch. Tretun Miss Matilda and Ch. Stoneacre Red Revenge
1992 Ch. Kelloe White Glove
1993 Ch. Kelloe White Glove
1994 Ch. Kelloe White Glove
1995 Ch. Kelloe White Glove
1996 Ch. Medbull Gold Dust over Kelloe
1997 Ch. Delrousher Fantasy Delight

Useful Addresses

Kennel Clubs

American Kennel Club Inc.
51 Madison Avenue
New York
NY10010
USA
Tel. 212/696 8329

Australian National Kennel Council
PO Box 285
Red Hill South
Victoria 3937
Australia
Tel. 00-61/015 304 338

Irish Kennel Club
Fotterell House
Greenmount Office Park
Dublin 6
Tel. 00 353 533 300

The Kennel Club (UK)
1–5 Clarges Street
Piccadilly
London
W1Y 8AB
UK
Tel. 0171 493 6651

FCI, Federation Cynologique Internationale
12 Rue Leopold II
B-6530 Thuin
Belgium

Société Centrale Canine
155 Avenue Jean Jaures
93535 Aubervilliers
CEDEX
France
Tel. 00 33 1 49 37 54 00

Verband fur das Deutsche Hundeween e.V.
Westfalendamm 174
D-4600
Dortmund
Germany
Tel. 00 49 231 56500-0

Breed Clubs and Organizations

United Kingdom

The Bulldog Breed Council

Secretary and Liaison Officer:
Mr Arthur Rowe
Burnside
Thurstonfield
Carlisle
Cumbria CA5 6HG
Tel. 01228 576424

Chairman:
Mr Robin Searle
Stannington Kennels
Morpeth
Northumberland
NE61 63J
Tel. 01670 789640

The following breed clubs are listed in alphabetical order. The date of each club's foundation is given after its name. An asterisk before the name indicates that club's membership of the Breed Council.

* Bath and Western Bulldog Club (1950)
Secretary: Mrs Sandra Davies
56 Tostrey
Hollybush
Cwmbran
Gwent NP44 7JD
Tel. 01633 864248

* Birmingham and Midland Counties Bulldog Club (1894)
Secretary: Mr Paul Hannah, JP
231 Hagley Green
Halesowen B63 1ED
Tel. 0121 550 4394

* Blackpool and Fylde Bulldog Club (1926)
Secretary: Sandra Dickinson
13 Pickup Street
Accrington
Lancashire BB5 0EY
Tel. 01254 397392

* British Bulldog Club (1892)
Secretary: Mr Les Thorpe
Longside Villa
Pilham
Nr Gainsborough
Lincolnshire DN21 3NU
Tel. 01427 628337

The Bulldog Club (Incorporated) (1875)
(*Registered in England No. 41170*)
Secretary: Mrs Maggie Story
73 St Neots Road
Hardwick
Cambridgeshire CB3 7QH
Tel. 01954 210226

* The Bulldog Club of Scotland (1926)
Secretary: Mrs Susan Rowe
Burnside
Thurstonfield
Carlisle

Cumbria CA5 6HG
Tel. 01228 576424

* Bulldog Club of Wales (1939)
Secretary: Mr J. Lane
16 WaunFach, Pentwyn
Cardiff CF2 7BA

* Caledonian Bulldog Club
    (1981)
Secretary: Mrs May Wyse
2 Muttonhall Cottage
Chaple Leval
Kirkcaldy
Fife
Tel. 01592 261017

* East Midland Bulldog Club
    (1966)
Secretary: Mr V. G. Haynes
The Orchard
Long Lane
Hickling
Melton Mowbray
Leicestershire LE14 3AG
Tel. 01664 822364

* Junior Bulldog Club (1912)
Secretary: Mrs Ginette Elliott
Marsbury
Whitehall Lane
Thorpe-le-Soken
Essex CO16 0AE
Tel. 01255 831248

* Leodensian Bulldog Club
    (1907)
Secretary: Mrs Viv Williams
19 Southend
Dunscroft
Doncaster DN7 4EJ

*London Bulldog Society (1891)
Secretary: Miss Susan Jay
5 Templeton Court
Radnor Walk
Shirley, Croydon
Surrey CR0 7NZ
Tel. 0181 777 0198

* Manchester and Counties
    Bulldog Club (1897)
Secretary: Mrs Margaret
    Williams
Crossroads Cottage
Chester Road, Dobshill
Flint CH5 3LZ
Tel. 01244 547226

* Northern Bulldog Club (1933)
Secretary: Mr Fred Haynes
129 Sunnyside Road
Droylsden
Manchester M35 7GF
Tel. 0161 301 4227

* Northumberland and Durham
    Bulldog Club (1899)
Secretary: Mrs Linda Robson
Chappark Cottage
Prestwick East Farm
Ponteland
Newcastle Upon Tyne NE20 9TX
Tel. 01661 871722

* Plymouth, Devon and
    Cornwall Bulldog Club (1929)
Secretary: Mrs Elaine Evely
Springfield Farm
Lutton
Nr. Ivybridge
Devon PL21 9RR
Tel. 01752 837354

* Rochdale and District Bulldog Club (1948)
Secretary: Mrs Annie Prescott
Brookhouse Farm
Chapel Lane
Sefton
Merseyside L30 7PD
Tel. 0151 531 8850

Sheffield and District Bulldog Club (1910)
Secretary: Mrs Anne
  Higginbottom
3 Worral Avenue
Treeton
Rotherham
South Yorkshire S60 5QG
Tel. 01742 694282

* South of England Bulldog Society (1946)
Secretary: Mrs L. Manns
Longacre
St Margarets Lane
Titchfield
Hampshire PO14 4BL
Tel. 01329 847005

*Yorkshire Bulldog Club (1905)
Secretary: Mr Ron Jones
232 Bradford Road
Tingley
Wakefield
West Yorkshire WF3 1RX
Tel. 01532 525430

United States of America

The Bulldog Club of America (BCA) consists of eight regional divisions, each with its own secretary:

Division I: Connecticut, Delaware, Maine, Massachusetts, New Hampshire, New Jersey, New York, Pennsylvania, Rhode Island, Vermont.
Division II: Illinois, Indiana, Kentucky, Michigan, Ohio, West Virginia, Wisconsin.
Division III: Arizona, California, Hawaii, Nevada.
Division IV: Arkansas, Colorado, Louisiana, New Mexico, Oklahoma, Texas, Utah, Wyoming.
Division V: Alaska, Idaho, Montana, Washington.
Division VI: Iowa, Kansas, Minnesota, Missouri, Nebraska, North Dakota, South Dakota.
Division VII: District of Colombia, Maryland, North Carolina, South Carolina, Virginia.
Division VIII: Alabama, Florida, Georgia, Mississippi, Tennessee.

Division I:
Secretary: Jean Kozatek
98 Brown Street
So. Attleboro
MA 02703
Tel. (503) 399 8647

Division II:
Secretary: Chris Knopf
PO Box 249
Shepherdsville
KY 40165
Tel. (502) 543 1772

Division III:
Secretary: Jack Kittrell
42236 20th Street
Lancaster
CA 93534
Tel. (805) 943 3330

Division IV:
Secretary: Brenda Newcombe
Rt. 4 Box 144
Elk City
OK 73644
Tel. (580) 225 3441

Division V:
Secretary: Ann Locke
2315 SW 219th Avenue
Hillsboro
OR 97123
Tel. (503) 591 0661

Division VI:
Secretary: Jo Hanson
6942 Morgan Avenue N.
Brooklyn Center
MN 55430
Tel. (612) 561 8265

Division VII:
Secretary: Dennis Quinn
PO Box 128
Sealston
VA 22547
Tel. (540) 775 2126

Division VIII:
Secretary: Nancy Isakson
1514 SW 12th Court
Fort Lauderdale
FL 33312
Tel. (954) 523 5514

Canada

**The Bulldog Club of Central
   Canada**
Secretary: Mrs Joan Vicar
P. O. Box 986

Kempville
Ontario
K0G 1GO

Australia

**Australian National British Bull-
   dog Breed Council (ANBBC)**
Secretary: Mrs Jean Turton
29a Phyllis St.
Mt. Pritchard

New South Wales 2170
Tel. 62-2-9602-6985
Website. http://www.flex.
   com.au/~buldawg/. E-mail.
   buldawg@flex.com.au

All state clubs are members of the Australian National British Bulldog Breed Council, with the exception of Queensland.

Queensland Bulldog Club
Secretary: Andrew Morris
P. O. Box 28
Landsborough, 4550
Tel. 07-5494-1029

Northern British Bulldog Club of New South Wales
Secretary: Mrs Michelle Partridge
20 Sophia Jane Avenue
Woodberry, 2322
Tel: 02-4966-1605

British Bulldog Club of New South Wales
Secretary: Mrs Jean Turton
(Address as ANBBC, *see* above)

British Bulldog Club of Southern Australia (Inc.)
Secretary: Mrs F. Barry
Lot 35A Dalkeith Road

Kudla
SA 5115
Tel. 08-8254-7159

British Bulldog Club of Tasmania
Secretary: Mrs Fran Smith
7 Schaw Street
Richmond
Tasmania 7025
Tel. 03-6260-2294

The British Bulldog Club of Victoria
Secretary: Mrs Sue Sherman
5 Hilaire Place
Whittlesea
Victoria 3757
Tel. 03-9716-1544

The British Bulldog Club of Western Australia
Secretary: Mrs Pauline Hales
2 Lissiman Street
Gosnells 6110
Tel. 09-490-2425

New Zealand

Southern Bulldog Club of New Zealand

Website.
http://www.es.co.nz/ ~blairdon/sbc/SBCP7.html.

Europe

Czech Republic: The Czech Bulldog Club
Mr Michel Korynta
110 00 Praha 1
Opatovicka 24
Tel. 00 4202 24917081

Fax. 00 4202 24914452

France: Club du Bulldog Anglais
Madame Helene Denis
25 rue des Carrieteres

57865 Amanvillers
Tel. 00 33 87 53 42 79
Fax. 00 33 87 53 54 70
E-mail. clubulldog@aol.com
Website.
http://members.aol.com/
clubulldog/homepage/
clubbull.htm

Italy:
  Circolo Italiano Bulldog
Riccardo Guiria
Via Bertieri 4
12073 CEVA (Cn)
Tel. 00 39 0174 785344
Fax. 00 39 0174 721532
E-mail. cib@segnografico.it
Website. http://www.
segnografico.it/cib/
bulldog.ht

Norway:
  The Bulldog Club of Norway
Secretary: Anne Haglund
Grindveien 16
N-1640 Rade
Norway

Tel. 47-63-85-02-53
President: Stale Blomhoff
Mosserudsveien 16
N-1969 Loken
Norway
Tel. 47-63-85-02-53

**Portugal: The Bulldog Club
  of Portugal**
Mrs Eva Koch
Magdala House
Azinhaga da Eira
Alcoitao
2765 Estoril
Tel. 00 351 460 0684
Fax. 00 351 460 0750
E-mail. magdala@mail.
telepac.pt

**Spain: Club Español del
  Bulldog Ingles**
Peter Frantzen
C/Jesus, 52
03578 Relleu/Alicante
Tel/Fax. 00 34 96 5619088
E-mail. vpy@CTV.ES

Newspapers and Magazines

Dog World (weekly)
Publisher: Dog World Ltd
9 Tufton Street
Ashford
Kent TN23 1QN
Tel. 01233 621877
Fax. 01233 645669
E-mail. Editorial@dogworld.co.uk

Our Dogs (weekly)
Publisher: Our Dogs Ltd
5 Oxford Road
Station Approach
Manchester M60 1SX
Tel. 0161 228 1984
Fax. 0161 236 0892
Website. http://www.k9.
co.uk/ourdogs

The Bulldog (Bi-annual)
Publisher: The Bulldog Club
(Incorporated)
Editor: Mrs Maggie Story
73 St Neots Road
Hardwick
Cambridge CB3 7QH
Te. 01954 210226
Website. http://www.K9netuk.
com/breedbulldogci.html.

Many of the UK breed clubs produce their own periodicals, hand-
books or newsheets.

The Bulldogger
Publisher:
The Bulldog Club of America
Co-editor: Ray Knudson
4300 Town Road
Salem
W1 53168
Tel/Fax. (414) 537 2771
Co-editor: Gene H. Cormick
P. O. Box 51
32W157 Glos Street
Wayne
IL 60184
Tel. (708) 377 7874

Bulldogs on the Internet

Breeders and fanciers can freely exchange information and views, and subscribe to an information mailing list, via the Internet. There is no fee. Send the message: sub-scribebulldogx-1 (immediately followed by your E-mail address) to: majordomo@io.com.

The *Wimsey Homepage* site has been compiled by Beth and Phil Handrick. It contains photographs and five-generation pedigrees of over 500 UK-bred Bulldogs, including the past winners of The Bulldog Club Inc. Champi-onship Show, Crufts and Bulldog of the Year. A 'CompuPed' database is available, and this contains over 13,000 UK-bred Bulldogs. Access the website on http://bluepost.tcimet.net/wimsey/

The Bulldog Club of America (BCA) has videos on gait, and publishes the excellent *Illustrated Guide to the Official Standard* (1995). Website: http://sculptor.as.arizona.edu/foltz/BCA/vidcaps/clip1ind.avi. The BCA itself has a separate website: http://thebca.org/ilstd.html

Index